gorgeous GLASS

20 sparkling ideas for painting on glass and china

20 sparkling ideas
for painting on
glass and china

gorgeous GLASS

Arlene Swiatek Gillen

 North Light Books, Cincinnati, Ohio
www.artistsnetwork.com

Gorgeous Glass: 20 Sparkling Ideas for Painting on Glass and China.
Copyright © 2008 by Arlene Swiatek Gillen. Manufactured in China. All rights reserved.
No part of this book may be reproduced in any form or by any electronic or mechanical
means including information storage and retrieval systems without permission in writing
from the publisher, except by a reviewer who may quote brief passages in a review.
The content of this book has been thoroughly reviewed for accuracy. However, the
author and publisher disclaim any liability for any damages, losses or injuries that may
result from the use or misuse of any product or information presented herein. It is the
purchaser's responsibility to read and follow all instructions and warnings on all product
labels. Published by North Light Books, an imprint of F+W Publications, Inc., 4700 East
Galbraith Road, Cincinnati, Ohio, 45236. (800) 289-0963. First Edition.

fw
www.fwbookstore.com

Other fine North Light Books are available from your local bookstore,
art supply store or direct from the publisher.

12   11   10   09   08   5   4   3   2   1

Distributed in Canada by Fraser Direct
100 Armstrong Avenue
Georgetown, ON, Canada L7G 5S4
Tel: (905) 877-4411

Distributed in the U.K. and Europe by David & Charles
Brunel House, Newton Abbot, Devon, TQ12 4PU, England
Tel: (+44) 1626 323200, Fax: (+44) 1626 323319
Email: postmaster@davidandcharles.co.uk

Distributed in Australia by Capricorn Link
P.O. Box 704, S. Windsor NSW, 2756 Australia
Tel: (02) 4577-3555

Library of Congress Cataloging-in-Publication Data

Gillen, Arlene Swiatek
    Gorgeous glass: 20 sparkling ideas for painting on glass and china /
Arlene Swiatek Gillen. -- 1st ed.
        p. cm
    Includes index.
    ISBN 978-1-60061-006-6 (pbk. : alk. paper)
  1. Glass craft. 2. Glass painting and staining. 3. Pottery craft. 4. China
painting--Technique. I. Title. II. Title: 20 sparkling ideas for painting on
glass and china. III. Title: Twenty sparkling ideas for painting on glass
and china.
TT298.G553 2008
748.5--dc22
                                          2007038251

Edited by Kathy Kipp
Design by Clare Finney
Production coordinated by Greg Nock
Photographed by Christine Polomsky and Tim Grondin
Photo styling by Louis Rub, Nora Fink and Leslie Brinkley

METRIC CONVERSION CHART		
To convert	to	multiply by
Inches	Centimeters	2.54
Centimeters	Inches	0.4
Feet	Centimeters	30.5
Centimeters	Foot	0.03
Yards	Meters	0.9
Meters	Yards	1.1

Photo by Gordon James Image Makers

ABOUT THE AUTHOR

Arlene Swiatek Gillen signed up for a beginner's decorative painting class in 1995 and by 1998 she was selling her painted furniture and home décor items at juried art festivals. Her handpainted wine glasses were best sellers and she began producing a line of wine glasses for gift shops and wineries. She started teaching the following year, first locally, then travel and convention teaching (SDP, New England Traditions, Kaswood, Creative Painting and MAD Painting). She has been a frequent contributor to the major decorative painting magazines. Her association with an interior designer led to commission work that included floral designs on walls, furniture and floor-cloths. Arlene is a member of the Society of Decorative Painters and the Buffalo Snowbirds Chapter. In 2004, she was honored to attend a reception hosted by First Lady Laura Bush and to see her handpainted ornament displayed on the White House Christmas tree. Arlene and her husband, Al, live in a century-old home in the friendly pastoral town of Holland, NY. She enjoys collecting antiques, gourmet cooking, gardening and traveling, especially the 5-star week-ends in Philadelphia with son Kevin, and visiting with son Brian and daughter-in-law Eleonora in Europe. You may reach Arlene at Arlene.Gillen@roadrunner.com.

DEDICATION

To Kevin and Brian, and Eleonora, who introduce me to the unfamiliar and exotic, lead me on adventures that expand my world and who fill my life with joy. And to my dear Amy, for all the flamingos.

ACKNOWLEDGMENTS

A sincere "Thank you" to my editor Kathy Kipp, who approached me about writing this book and whose vision, enthusiasm and expertise made this an exciting and enjoyable collaboration, and to photographer Christine Polomsky, whose skill with the camera and computer is truly impressive.

contents

20 STEP-BY-STEP PROJECTS
YOU CAN PAINT

introduction

I'm happy painting on just about any surface, but painting on glass and china certainly holds special appeal. There is essentially no surface preparation—just clean and go! In most instances, transferring a pattern to the glass or china surface is not necessary. The pattern may be copied onto white bond paper, cut out, and placed inside or behind the glass. Some of the designs in this book are painted without a pattern; simple templates or masking tape are used instead. This allows you the option of adapting my designs to your choice of surface. And, your choices are almost unlimited. You'll find unique glassware and china at craft stores, department and discount stores, on the internet and even at garage and estate sales.

You may want to add some very special touches to your table with projects that combine glassware with other painted surfaces. You'll find instructions for a set of crimson napkins that coordinate with a pair of vintage red glass goblets. And there are summer beverage glasses with canvas coasters painted with pink geraniums. If you are really ambitious and love detailed designs, you'll enjoy painting the porcelain place settings and matching napkin rings to use for those special occasion dinners.

I hope these designs will inspire your own creativity and that you experience the pleasure of creating and sharing that which is beautiful, unique and personal.

materials

PAINTS

All the projects in this book were painted with Plaid FolkArt Paints. Enamels were used for glass and china surfaces; acrylics were used for all other surfaces.

MEDIUMS

Clear Medium is used to add transparency to the enamel paints and is also used as the floating medium; Flow Medium is used to thin the enamels since water may not be added to them; Extender is used to keep the enamels moist for a longer period of time.

BRUSH CLEANING SUPPLIES

To clean your brushes after painting, fill the compartments of a Loew-Cornell Brush Tub with 1½-inches (3.8cm) of clean water. Pull the ferrule of the brush across the ribs in the bottom of the brush tub several times; the vibration will loosen any paint that may have gotten up into the ferrule. Use your fingers to gently work a little brush cleaner or mild dishwashing liquid into the bristles and repeat. Finally, rinse the brush in the clean water compartment.

GENERAL PAINTING SUPPLIES

Isopropyl alcohol 70% (rubbing alcohol): Use to clean your hands and the glass and china surfaces prior to painting to remove fingerprints and skin oils.

Palette knife: For mixing paints on your palette.

Palette paper: This is used as both your paint palette and blending palette.

Tracing paper: Place this over the patterns in this book and trace the design.

White or gray transfer paper: Place this face down

(Shown below) Palette knife, palette paper, tracing paper, white and gray transfer paper, condiment cups, wooden skewers and brush tub.

under your traced design to transfer the pattern to bond paper or to the painting surface. Use white transfer paper for dark surfaces; use gray for bond paper and light surfaces.

Paper towels: Use good quality paper towels, such as Viva or Bounty, for cleaning your glassware with alcohol and for wicking moisture from your brushes before loading with enamels.

Condiment cups: Enamels dry quickly on your palette. Covering your paint puddles with these plastic cups will help keep the paint moist a bit longer.

Wooden or bamboo skewers: Once the paint has dried to the touch, small errors may be scraped from the glass or china surface with the pointed tip of the skewer.

FolkArt blank adhesive stencil, cotton swabs (regular and baby protector), Krylon Matte Finish Spray No. 1311, and EtchAll Dip 'n Etch.

SUPPLIES FOR SPECIFIC PROJECTS

Plaid Blank Adhesive Stencil: Use this for the apple and pear shapes that are reverse-painted on glass plates.

Krylon 18 Kt. Gold Leafing Pen: The chisel point is used to apply a fine gold edge to the Pink Geranium canvas coasters.

Spongit Sticks: Perfect for applying color to the rims of plates and chargers.

Cotton swabs (regular and baby protector swabs) and sponge-tipped detail painters: Use for basecoating small round shapes such as blueberries and small flowers.

Stylus: Use for dip dots.

Medium grit sandpaper: Use this only on the herb tiles. A light sanding will scuff the surface and aid the adhesion of the acrylic paints.

EtchAll Dip 'n Etch etching fluid: Immerse bottles, glasses, etc., in this solution to achieve an etched or frosted-glass surface.

Krylon Matte Finish Spray No. 1311: Seals the background painting on porous tile before the decorative design is added.

Blue painter's tape & 1/4-inch (6mm) masking tape: The painter's tape is used to protect the surface when paint is applied to adjacent areas; the masking tape is used as a straight edge for painting stripes.

Small T-square: Use this to obtain perfect 45° angles when taping off the herb tiles before the faux antiquing is applied.

China marker: A dark color china marker is used for placing marks on glass and china for pattern placement.

Sharpie pen: Patterns drawn with an ultrafine-point Sharpie pen are clearly visible when placed behind cobalt or red glassware.

X-Acto knife: Use the sharp point of the knife to cleanly cut out the fruit shapes from the adhesive stencil material.

Small tape measure: A flexible tape measure works well when measuring for pattern placement, especially on rounded surfaces such as cruets.

(Left to right) Small and large detail painters, Loew-Cornell Spongit Stick, Krylon 18 Kt. Gold Leafing Pen, Stylus.

BRUSHES

I used Loew-Cornell Golden Taklon brushes for the projects in this book. There is a perfect "spring" to the bristles and, with proper cleaning and care, the brushes hold their points and fine chisel edges very well. From top to bottom:

Scumbler (Series 2014): a natural bristle brush used for stippling.

Liner (Series 7350 and Series JS): use the mid-length JS liner for fine linework such as vines and striping; use the regular 7350 liner for fine details such as highlights on small berries.

Filbert (Series 7500): my most frequently used brush. An innovative double loading technique makes quick work of painting hydrangeas and geraniums.

Shader (Series 7300): a flat brush with a chisel edge; perfect for rose petals, leaves and sideload floats.

Ultra Round (Series 7020): has the fullness of a round brush but the fine point of a liner. Use with thinned paint for vines and tendrils.

Round (Series 7000): the tip of this brush fans out with very little pressure and then springs back to a point for daisy petals and stroke work.

10 tips for glass painting success

- Your hands and the painting surface must be impeccably clean. Avoid touching the painting area after you have cleaned the surface with rubbing alcohol and a soft paper towel.

- Use a poly-coated paper palette for your paints. This comes in a pad of forty 9 x 12-inch (22.9 x 30.5 cm) disposable sheets.

- Enamels dry quickly on your palette. Keeping paint puddles covered with little plastic condiment cups will keep the paint fresher longer.

- Do not introduce any water into the Plaid FolkArt Enamels. After rinsing brushes in water, wick as much moisture as possible from the bristles by pressing them between paper towels before loading in paint.

- Paint with a fully loaded brush and a light touch. A fully loaded brush should have paint three-fourths of the way up the bristles.

- Clear Medium, Flow Medium and Extender are used in place of water for specific techniques, such as sideload floats, thinning paint for line work and details, striping and dip dots.

- Allow each layer of paint to dry before adding highlights, shading and details. A small portable hair dryer may be used to force-dry the paint, but allow the surface to cool before continuing.

- A little variation in the painted design is desirable; this makes each piece unique.

- Follow the directions on the paint bottles for curing the paint. Enamels are still a little tender after they dry and before they are fully cured, so handle your painted pieces carefully.

- Although the enamel paints are top-shelf dishwasher-safe, I recommend washing your painted glass and china by hand, just as you would any fine crystal or china.

PUTTING PAINT ON YOUR PALETTE

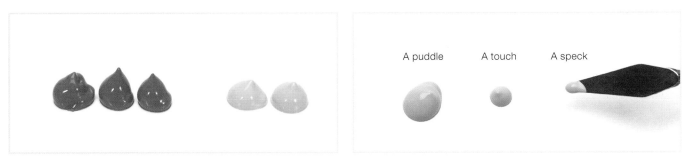

When you are placing paint colors on your palette to make color mixes for the projects in this book, use the "chocolate chip" method. Place a puddle of paint the size of a chocolate chip on your palette. If the instructions say "mix green and yellow 3:2," that means the ratio for the color mix is 3 parts green to 2 parts yellow, so you will place 3 green chips and 2 yellow chips on your palette and mix them together.

A puddle   A touch   A speck

What is the difference between a puddle, a touch, and a speck of color? When you are mixing paints, a "puddle" is about the size of a chocolate chip; a "touch" means adding less than a measurable ratio of one color to another. To add a "speck," use the point of a palette knife to pick up and add one color to another color.

DOUBLE LOADING A SHADER OR FLAT BRUSH—TRADITIONAL METHOD

1 Here is the standard, traditional way of double-loading a flat or shader. First, dip one corner of the brush in your first color.

2 Load the other corner of the flat or shader into your second color. This is how your brush will look if you have double-loaded it correctly.

3 Blend on your palette paper and then paint the stroke. You can see how the two colors blend seamlessly across the stroke.

DOUBLE LOADING A FILBERT OR FLAT BRUSH—NON-TRADITIONAL METHOD

1 Create a small loading zone in each puddle of paint with the palette knife. Load one flat side of the brush by gently pressing and pulling the brush in the first loading zone. Note the low angle of the brush.

2 Flip the brush over, place the other flat side of the brush in the loading zone of the second color, and gently press and pull to load the paint.

3 Hold the brush so the first color (here it's the light lavender) is next to the surface, and pull your stroke. Both colors will show, but the second color (here it's the dark plum) will dominate.

DOUBLE LOADING A LINER BRUSH

1 To double load a liner brush, pull the long bristles across the top of the puddle of your first color.

2 Flip the liner over and pull the clean side of the bristles across the top of the puddle of the second color. Note that you should not dip the brush into the paint puddle when you are double loading.

3 If you have double loaded correctly, both colors should be clearly seen on the liner.

CREATING A SIDELOAD FLOAT

1 For sideload floats, always dress the brush in Clear Medium first. Pick up a small amount of Clear Medium on the flat shader and work it into the brush by stroking on your palette paper.

2 Load one corner of the brush into your paint color.

3 Blend the paint into the medium by pulling short strokes as you move first to the left, then flip the brush over and stroke to the right, taking care to maintain a clean edge on the brush.

4 The sideload float should be darkest on one edge and fade to nothing in the center and the other edge. If any color is showing on the other edge, you may have loaded too much paint on the corner, or you may have let the color travel across the bristles as you blended. Since sideload floats are most often used to shade or add shadows, it's important that the color fade away subtly and gradually, without any hard or abrupt edges.

BASIC BRUSHSTROKES

Open-crescent and closed-crescent strokes: For the open crescent, begin with the flat shader on the chisel edge, apply pressure as you slide the brush up and around, then release pressure and end the stroke on the chisel edge. For the closed crescent, begin on the chisel edge, apply pressure as you pivot and lift the brush back up to the chisel edge; the bottom corner of the brush stays in the same spot.

Comma stroke and straight comma: Press the round brush to the surface to allow the bristles to fan out, pull the stroke as you release pressure on the brush allowing the bristles to return to a point at the tail end of the stroke.

Modified "S" stroke for ribbons and leaves: Slide the flat shader on its chisel edge, apply pressure and slide the brush back up to its chisel edge. Connect several of these strokes to achieve the look of twisting ribbons and leaves.

FAN STROKE

1 Fully load the round brush in orange, then pick up peach on the point of the brush. Place the brush on the surface and apply pressure by leaning the handle of the brush slightly forward and rotating the handle ever so slightly from left to right to fan out the bristles.

2 Lift the ferrule just off the surface and push the bristles forward about 1/8 inch (3mm).

3 Pull the brush back, ending the stroke on the point of the brush.

DIP DOTS WITH A STYLUS

The easiest way to make nice round dots is by using a stylus. These tools come with different sizes of ball tips. Load the stylus by touching the tip to the paint puddle. Use a fine stylus for tiny pollen dots, a medium stylus for dip dot accents, and a large stylus for flower centers.

FIVE EASY LEAF STROKES

Single stroke leaf: Double load a flat shader with a dark and a light green. Begin on the chisel edge of the brush, apply pressure and slide forward, lifting to the chisel edge and coming to a point.

Heart-shaped leaf: Double load a filbert brush with a dark and a light green. Paint two side-by-side comma strokes, overlapping the second over the first at the base.

Comma stroke leaves: Use a mid-length liner to paint a single comma stroke, then add another comma stroke on each side.

Two-stroke leaves (plain & ruffled): Begin the first stroke on the chisel edge of the flat shader, apply pressure so that the bristles fan out to the left and slide the brush back up to its chisel edge; rotate your surface and place the corner of the brush at the bottom corner of the first stroke, apply pressure as you slide the brush back up to the chisel edge to form the point of the leaf. Do the same for the ruffled leaf, but apply and release pressure on the brush as you slide the brush back up to the chisel edge.

Traditional double-loaded plain and ruffled leaves: Load one corner of the flat shader in light green, the other corner in dark green and blend on palette paper. Paint the strokes so that the colors will alternate on the leaf.

FLOWER PETALS

Four-petal flower using a non-traditional double-loaded filbert: Double load a filbert in a light blue and a dark blue as shown on page 13. With the light blue toward the surface, paint the top center petal first, then the left and right petals. Paint the bottom petal left to right with the chisel edge of the brush.

Five-petal flowers using a flat shader: To paint five-petal flowers with evenly spaced petals, paint the first three petals in the order shown to form an upside down "Y" shape, then add the remaining two petals in the order shown. Use a stylus or small round brush to dot the center of the flower.

COMPARING COLORS WHEN MIXING

If you need to mix more paint of a particular color, leave some of the original paint mix on your palette so that you can compare the new mix to the original mix for accuracy.

OFF-LOADING PAINT FROM A STIPPLER

The scumbler is used for reverse painting on glass plates with the aid of stencils. To achieve a lacy effect, load the brush in paint, then offload by rubbing the brush in a circular motion on a pad of clean, dry paper towels.

FIXING MISTAKES WITH A WOODEN OR BAMBOO SKEWER

1 Glass and china are slick surfaces and occasionally a stroke may not be finished off as neatly as desired, such as the upper tip of this leaf.

2 When the paint has dried to the touch, you may use the point of a wooden or bamboo skewer to scrape off any untidy edges without harming the glass or china surface.

PREPARING AND USING PATTERNS

1 In some of the projects in this book, you will be instructed to place a pattern into a wine glass or goblet. Because these surfaces may be rounded, you will need to make release cuts into the pattern on the broken lines to allow the pattern to conform to the shape of the glass.

2 After the release cuts are made, tape the ends of the pattern together.

3 Place the pattern into the glass and tape into place. Press the pattern against the surface of the glass; if needed, a crumpled paper towel or tissue paper may be used to keep the pattern pressed against the surface of the glass.

easy leaves on
juice glasses

materials

PAINTS
Cobalt
Italian Sage
Lemon Custard
Licorice
Periwinkle
Thicket

BRUSHES
no. 6 shader
no. 2 ultra round
no. 1 JS liner
nos. 2, 4 and 6 filberts

SURFACES
Set of 4 "Strobe" 7-oz. juice
glasses, available at Bed Bath
& Beyond. Similar glassware
can be found at home centers
and department stores.

ADDITIONAL SUPPLIES
Flow Medium
Stylus

Let's begin with a quick and easy project painted on four small juice glasses. A simple leaf-and-vine design encircles the outside of each glass. If you have never painted on glass, this is a good place to start. You'll experience the "feel" of using different brushes on the slick glass surface and gain the confidence to move on to other projects in this book. There are four different kinds of leaves to paint in this project, starting with a simple single-stroke leaf and moving on to heart-shaped leaves, ruffled-edge leaves and comma stroke leaves. Choose your favorite or paint all four!

COLOR MIXES

LIGHT GREEN MIX:
Italian Sage + a touch
of Lemon Custard

DARK GREEN MIX:
Thicket + a touch of
Licorice

BLUE MIX:
Periwinkle + a touch
of Cobalt

patterns

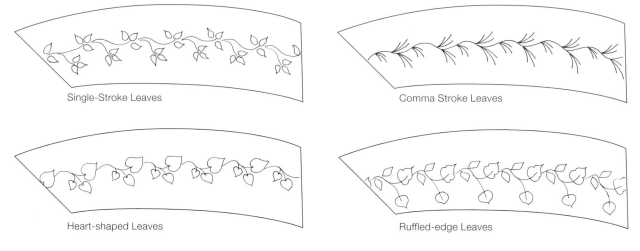

Single-Stroke Leaves

Comma Stroke Leaves

Heart-shaped Leaves

Ruffled-edge Leaves

These patterns may be hand-traced or photocopied for personal use only. Enlarge at 200%, then at 132% to bring them up to full size.

PLACEMENT OF DESIGNS

Place each pattern inside the glass so the leaf-and-vine design is about one inch (25mm) below the rim of the glass. This creates a consistent look across all four glasses.

SINGLE-STROKE LEAVES

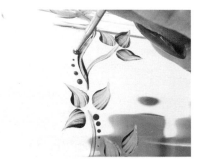

1 Load a no. 4 filbert with Italian Sage + a touch of Lemon Custard on one side of the brush, and Thicket + a touch of Licorice on the other side. With the lighter green side of the brush toward the glass, form each leaf with one single stroke. Re-load your brush for every leaf.

2 Pull a little of the dark green paint out of the puddle on your palette and thin it with a few drops of Flow Medium. Use a no. 2 ultra round to paint the vine. Aim the vine toward the center of each three-leaf cluster. Remove the pattern.

3 The blue dip-dots are made with a stylus. Mix a blue of Periwinkle + a touch of Cobalt + a drop of Flow Medium. The largest dot is next to the leaf; the dots get smaller as you go along the vine. Wipe off the stylus on a paper towel after each series of dots, and re-load. Let dry.

HEART-SHAPED LEAVES

 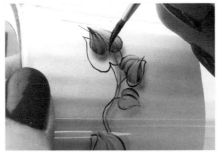 

1 With the same colors used for the single-stroke leaves, start with the largest leaves and paint two side-by-side short comma strokes with a no. 6 filbert. Switch to a no. 4 filbert for the next smaller leaves, then a no. 2 for the smallest leaves.

2 Pull a little of the dark green paint out of the puddle on your palette and thin it with a few drops of Flow Medium. Use a no. 2 ultra round to paint the vine. Aim the vine toward the center of each leaf.

3 Remove the pattern and paint the blue dip-dots with the same color and stylus as for the single stroke leaves. Let dry.

RUFFLED-EDGE LEAVES

1 Use the same greens and a traditional double load on a no. 6 shader. Pull the ruffled-edge side of the leaf first, keeping the Thicket to the outside edge of the leaf. Without flipping your brush over, paint the second half of the leaf so the Thicket creates the vein in the center.

2 Pull a little of the dark green paint out of the puddle on your palette and thin it with a few drops of Flow Medium. Use a no. 2 ultra round to paint the vine. For the smaller, single-stroke leaves in between the larger leaves, use the same two greens on a no. 6 shader.

3 Remove the pattern and paint the blue dip-dots with the same color and stylus as for the single stroke leaves. Let dry.

COMMA STROKE LEAVES

1 Scoop a little of the dark green paint into a separate puddle and thin with Flow Medium. Use a no. 2 ultra round brush and paint the vine first.

2 For the comma stroke leaves, load a no. 1 JS liner into the dark green mix, then pick up just a speck of the light green. Paint the long center stroke, wipe the brush on a paper towel, re-load, and paint the two shorter strokes. Always pull the stroke toward the vine.

3 Remove the pattern and paint the blue dip-dots with the same color and stylus as for the single stroke leaves. Let dry.

reverse-painted
bamboo plates

materials

PAINTS
Hauser Medium Green
Licorice
Sunflower
Thicket
Warm White

BRUSH
no. 6 shader

SURFACES
Square glass plates, 6¾ inches
(16.1cm), by Bormioli, available
at Linens-N-Things. Square
green and ivory ceramic chargers also available at Linens-
N-Things. Similar plates can
be found at home centers and
department stores.

ADDITIONAL SUPPLIES
Small plastic condiment cups
to cover the puddles of paint
on your palette to keep them
moist and fresh while you
paint.

These square glass plates make a great
surface on which to paint a simple bamboo design. Their shape
is fresh and contemporary while the bamboo design adds a
Zen-like quality to the table setting. "Reverse-painted" means
the bamboo is painted on the underside of the plates but viewed
from the front. For a coordinating teapot (shown below), use
gray transfer paper and a stylus to transfer sections of the pattern to the ceramic teapot. Use the same color mixes as for the
plates, but keep the dark green side of the flat brush toward the
surface when painting the leaves.

COLORS

LIGHT GREEN MIX:	DARK GREEN MIX:	MEDIUM GREEN MIX:	YELLOW-GREEN MIX:
Hauser Medium Green + Warm White 3:2	Thicket + a speck of Licorice	Light green mix + dark green mix 1:1	Sunflower + Hauser Medium Green 2:1

Adapt the
bamboo design
to a ceramic
teapot to coor-
dinate with your
glass plates.
This is a "teapot
for one," half
teapot and half
tea cup.

pattern

This pattern may be hand-traced or photocopied for personal use only. Enlarge at 164% to bring it up to full size. The leaves with the dotted lines are painted with a different brush loading technique than the ones with the solid lines. Refer to the instructions for details.

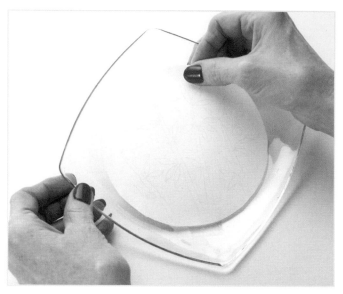

1 Trace the pattern onto a sheet of white bond paper. Cut into a circle following the circular line on the pattern. Tape the pattern face down to the front of the plate. Note that the direction of the bamboo canes goes from corner to corner on the plate.

2 Turn the plate over. This is how the pattern looks as seen through the back of the glass. You will be able to follow the pattern easily as you paint on the back of the plate.

3 Mix 3 parts of Hauser Medium Green + 2 parts of Warm White for a light green. Mix Thicket + a speck of Licorice for a dark green. Load a no. 6 shader with the light green mix and tip into the dark green mix. Start at the top of the bamboo canes in the center. Touch the chisel edge of the brush to the glass, press down, and rotate the brush as you pull downward to paint the uppermost segment of the cane.

4 Paint the next segments with the flat side of the brush. The Thicket that's on your brush forms the growth segment. To paint the two outer canes, load the brush with a medium green mix of equal parts light and dark green mixes, then tip into the dark green.

5 Mix a yellow-green from 2 parts Sunflower and 1 part Hauser Medium Green. Paint the leaves indicated by the solid lines with medium green on one flat side of the shader, then alternate between using yellow-green mix and light green mix on the other side of the shader. This will give a natural-looking variation to the leaves. The light green and the yellow-green should always be toward the glass surface as you paint each leaf.

6 For the dotted-line leaves on the pattern, load your shader with dark green mix on one side and medium green on the other. Keep the dark green side toward the glass surface for each of these leaves.

7 This is how your reverse-painted plate looks from the back when you're finished painting and you've removed the pattern.

8 And this is how the plate looks from the front. Notice how the colors of the leaves look different from this side, depending on which green mix was facing the glass when you applied your brush. The way you load your brush gives you the natural striation in the leaves.

wisteria on
frosted glass

materials

PAINTS

Dioxazine Purple
Fresh Foliage
Hydrangea
Italian Sage
Lemon Custard
Licorice
Night Sky
Plum Vineyard
Pure Magenta
Thicket
Violet Pansy
Wicker White

BRUSHES

nos. 2 and 4 shaders
no. 1 JS liner

SURFACES

Clear glass bottles with stoppers in three different shapes, 4½ to 6 inches (11.5 to 15.2 cm) tall, available at Michaels and A.C. Moore

ADDITIONAL SUPPLIES

EtchAll Dip 'n Etch etching fluid
Flow Medium
Plastic container
China marker

The simple technique of frosting glass

adds a subtle elegance to inexpensive clear glass bottles. The bottles were immersed in etching fluid for 15 minutes and then rinsed in water (see page 29 for complete instructions). The chemical reaction transforms the shiny glass surface to a frosted satin finish that gives a lovely glow to these bottles. For each different shape of bottle I painted a different color of wisteria, from the classic purple to a light pink and a medium blue. The design is similar across all three bottles so try painting the complete set, then fill with your favorite colognes or bath salts.

COLOR MIXES

PURPLE MIX:
Violet Pansy +
Dioxazine Purple 4:1

LIGHT LAVENDER MIX:
Wicker White + a touch of Purple mix

DARK GREEN MIX:
Thicket + a speck of Licorice

LIGHT GREEN MIX:
Italian Sage + Lemon Custard 3:1

BRIGHT GREEN MIX:
Fresh Foliage + Wicker White 4:1

PLUM MIX:
Plum Vineyard + Pure Magenta 4:1

LIGHT PINK MIX:
Wicker White + a touch of Plum mix

DARK BLUE MIX:
Night Sky + a touch of Hydrangea

LIGHT BLUE MIX:
Wicker White + a touch of Dark Blue mix

patterns

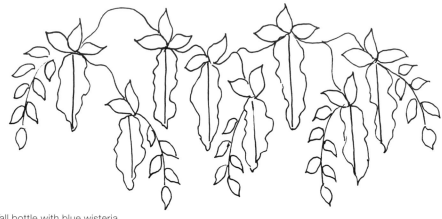

These patterns may be hand-traced or photocopied for personal use only. They are shown here at 100%.

Tall bottle with blue wisteria

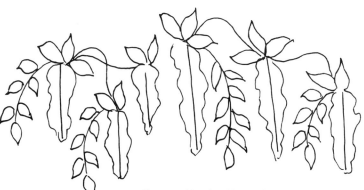

Short oval bottle with purple wisteria

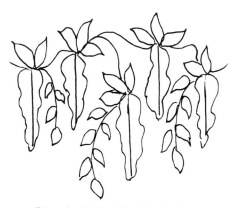

Triangular bottle with pink wisteria

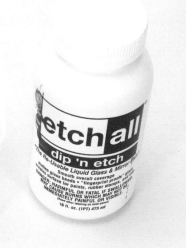

1 If you want to frost the outside of the bottles before painting on them, first gather your supplies: your glass bottle, a sturdy plastic container larger than the bottle, and EtchAll Dip 'n Etch etching fluid, which can be found at any craft store.

2 Fill the plastic container halfway with water. Fill the glass bottle with water to weight it down and place the bottle in the water. Add or remove water from the container until the waterline is where you want the top of the frosted area to be on the bottle.

3 Remove the bottle from the container. Use a china marker to mark the outside of the container with a line that's level with the height of the water.

4 Pour the water out of the plastic container and dry the container with a towel (be careful not to remove the level line you just drew on the outside!). Fill the container with Dip 'n Etch up to the line you marked on the outside. Place the weighted glass bottle down in the etching fluid and leave it there for 15 minutes.

5 Remove the bottle from the etching fluid, rinse under running water, and dry thoroughly. Pour the Dip 'n Etch back into its original jar—it can be reused over and over.

purple wisteria

1 Trace your pattern and use a piece of gray transfer paper and a stylus to transfer only the solid vertical lines of the centers of each wisteria blossom, as shown on the patterns.

2 Turn the bottle upside down to paint the petals. Mix 4 parts Violet Pansy + 1 part of Dioxazine Purple to make a purple mix. Add a touch of the purple mix to Wicker White to make a light lavender mix. Use a no. 2 shader and load one flat side in the purple and the other flat side in the lavender. With the lavender side toward the glass, paint tiny strokes starting at the pointed tip of the wisteria cluster and working toward the top of the cluster, widening out as you go.

3 Continue adding tiny strokes for the individual blossoms all the way to the top of the cluster. Turn the bottle right side up to check your work. Paint the other wisteria clusters the same way, re-loading your brush every three to four strokes.

4 Mix Thicket + a speck of Licorice to make a dark green. Mix 3 parts Italian Sage and 1 part Lemon Custard for a light green. Mix 4 parts Fresh Foliage and 1 part Wicker White to make a bright green. Double-load a no. 4 shader, one corner always in the dark green, the other corner in one of the other two greens. Blend a little on your palette. Paint the three-leaf clusters along the top, varying the colors by picking up light green sometimes and bright green other times. Keep the dark green corner of your brush always next to the wisteria blossom.

5 Pull out a little puddle of your dark green mix on your palette and thin it with Flow Medium. Use a no. 1 JS liner to paint the vine that connects the leaves of the wisteria clusters.

6 With the same brush and color, pull vines downward between the flower clusters. Using a no. 2 shader and the same greens as for the leaves, paint the tiny leaves on these vines. Re-load every two to three leaves.

7 You can use these same instructions and designs for other colors of wisteria. For this dark pink wisteria, mix 4 parts Plum Vineyard + 1 part Pure Magenta for a plum mix; for the light pink mix, add a touch of the plum mix to Wicker White.

8 The blue wisteria is painted with a mix of 2 parts Night Sky + a touch of Hydrangea for the dark blue; add a touch of this dark blue mix to Wicker White for the light blue mix.

french country
stemware

materials

PAINTS
Autumn Leaves
Berry Wine
Engine Red
Pure Orange
Thicket
Wicker White
Yellow Ochre

BRUSHES
no. 4 shader
no. 3 round
no. 1 JS liner
10/0 JS liner
no. 1 liner

SURFACES
Cobalt blue wine glasses
available only at www.target.
com. Similar blue glasses may
be found at home centers and
department stores.

ADDITIONAL SUPPLIES
Ultra Fine Point Sharpie Pen
Cotton "baby protector" swabs
Stylus
Clear Medium
Flow Medium

The bright primary colors of French country
are perfect for painting on a dark-colored glass such as cobalt
blue stemware. This project is a good example of how painted
glassware can add impact when used with coordinating table-
top pieces. I designed the rooster charger plate and the napkin
ring to work with the cobalt blue wine glasses, painting all of
them with a coordinating border design to complete the French
country look. Both the plate and the napkin ring are painted on
wooden surfaces using regular acrylic paints. Instructions and
patterns are available for these two items; please see "Where to
Find It" on page 126.

COLORS

Berry Wine Wicker White

COLOR MIXES

RED MIX:
Engine Red + Autumn
Leaves 2:1

PUMPKIN MIX:
Pure Orange + Yellow
Ochre 1:1

LIGHT YELLOW MIX:
Yellow Ochre + Wicker
White 4:1

**MEDIUM GREEN
MIX:**
Thicket + a touch of
Yellow Ochre

pattern

PREPARATION

Trace and transfer or photocopy the pattern onto white bond paper, then go over the transfer lines with an ultra fine point Sharpie pen. Cut out the pattern along the solid lines on all four sides, then cut into the pattern along the broken lines at top and bottom. These are called "release lines" because they allow the flat pattern to fit snugly within the curve of the wine glass. Butt the short edges of the pattern (don't overlap), tape them together and place the pattern into the glass. The top of the pattern should be even with the rim of the glass. Tape into place. Moisten your fingertips and carefully mold the pattern against the curved inside surface of the glass. This prevents distortion of the design as you paint.

This pattern may be hand-traced or photocopied for personal use only. Enlarge at 133% to bring it up to full size.

1 Load Wicker White onto a "baby-protector" cotton swab and basecoat the round shape of the flowers with a tapping motion. This opaque white undercoat will help the red paint show up better on the dark blue glass. Let the white dry completely before continuing. Prepare a red mix with 2 parts Engine Red and 1 part Autumn Leaves. Use another clean cotton swab to tap this red over the white undercoat of the flowers.

2 Dress a no. 4 shader in Clear Medium, sideload in Berry Wine, blend, and shade each red flower where it meets its stem. Also shade the throat, or bowl, of each red flower. For the highlights, mix equal parts Pure Orange and Yellow Ochre to create a pumpkin mix. Dress a no. 4 shader in Clear Medium, sideload into the pumpkin mix, blend, and float highlights along the top of the flower and the top of the throat.

3 Mix 4 parts Yellow Ochre and 1 part Wicker White plus a touch of Flow Medium to make a light yellow mix. Use the no. 1 JS liner to make the long curving strokes that arch over the red flowers. Use a no. 1 liner for the shorter connecting strokes and the three comma strokes. For the thin cross-hatching strokes, thin the yellow mix with more Flow Medium and use a 10/0 liner. Follow the shape of the shorter strokes to make your cross-hatch lines. Re-load your brush for every line.

4 For the stems and leaves, mix Thicket + a touch of Yellow Ochre to make a medium green. Load the no. 1 JS liner in the medium green, tip into the light yellow mix from step 3, and paint the flower stems. Load a no. 3 round brush in the medium green mix, tip into the yellow mix and paint the four comma-stroke leaves under the single red flower.

5 For the two S-stroke leaves on each side under the cluster of three red flowers, use a no. 4 shader. Load into the medium green mix, tip into the light yellow mix, and paint an S-stroke to form each leaf.

6 All the dip dots and pollen dots are made with the same light yellow mix from step 3 and a little Flow Medium. The pollen dots in the throat of each red flower are done with a very fine stylus. The dip dots under the cross-hatch design and at the base of the stems are done with a larger stylus. If you wish, paint a grouping of a single flower, three comma strokes and some dip dots on the base of each wine glass.

bridal lace
crystal flutes

materials

PAINTS
Pearl White Metallic
Wicker White

BRUSHES
nos. 4, 6 and 8 shaders
10/0 JS liner

SURFACE
Set of 2 crystal champagne
flutes, "Stephanie" by Mikasa.
Similar glassware can be found
at fine department stores.

ADDITIONAL SUPPLIES
Clear Medium
Flow Medium
Stylus
Colored tissue paper
China marker

What a lovely gift for the engaged

couple: toasting flutes for their wedding day and for every special celebration thereafter. The pearlescent white floral design is repeated three times around each crystal champagne flute. The designs are then connected with flowing ribbons of sheer white paint. When painting the floral design, have a generous amount of paint on one corner of your brush; this will form a slight ridge on the edges of the petals and leaves and add texture and dimension to the design.

COLORS

PEARL WHITE MIX:
Pearl White Metallic +
Wicker White 4:1

pattern

Complete pattern

Direction of roses

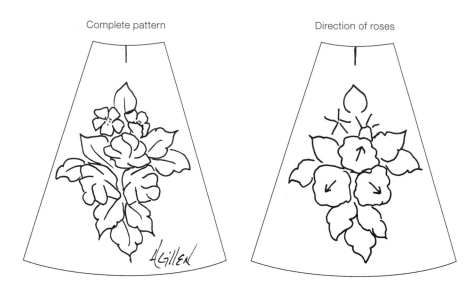

Positioning template

These patterns may be hand-traced or photocopied for personal use only. Enlarge the rose patterns at 125% and the positioning template at 143% to bring them up to full size. Transfer the patterns onto a sheet of colored bond paper and cut them out.

The pattern on the far left shows all the details of the roses, leaves and filler flowers. The arrows on the pattern at near left show the direction each full rose should face. In this project I am using this pattern taped inside the crystal flute for my painting guide; I will refer to the other pattern only for the placement of the details.

PREPARATION
Because the finished painting is translucent, none of the elements of the design, such as the leaves and roses, overlap; they're just placed next to each other. You'll start in the center of the design and work your way outward.

1 To use the "positioning template," cut it out and tape the ends together to make a circle. Place the template over the outside of the top of the glass. Use a china marker to make a registration mark on the glass above each vertical line. You will use this to line up the centerline of the pattern.

2 Remove the positioning template and slip one of the design patterns inside the glass, line up the top of the pattern with the top of the glass, align the registration mark with the centerline on the pattern, and place a piece of tape over the rim to secure the pattern in place. Place a crumpled piece of tissue paper or paper towel inside to press the pattern up against the inside of the glass. Remove the little line made by the china marker.

PAINT THE ROSE PETALS IN THIS ORDER

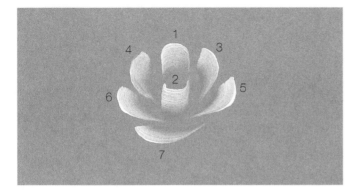

This is an "exploded" view of the white rose you'll be painting. The petals are moved apart so you can clearly see their shape and where they fit together. The numbers tell you in which order to paint each petal. The step-by-step photos below show the rose being painted on the glass with the pattern inside.

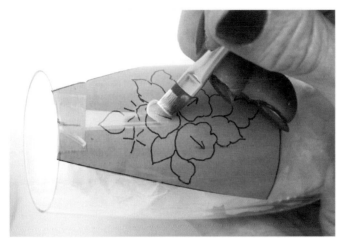

1 Mix 4 parts Pearl White Metallic + 1 part Wicker White to make a pearl white mix. This is the only color you'll use throughout. Pick up Clear Medium on one corner of a no. 8 shader. Blend slightly on your palette, taking care to maintain a clean corner on your brush. Now pick up some pearl white mix on the clean corner, blend on the palette, and paint the top back petal of the rose with the paint corner of the brush at the edge of the petal.

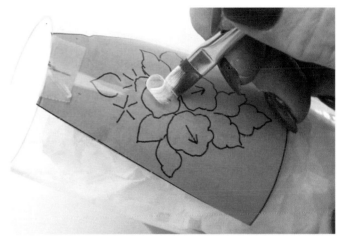

2 Re-load your brush. Paint the front of the cup of the rose, keeping the paint corner of the brush at the top edge of the petal.

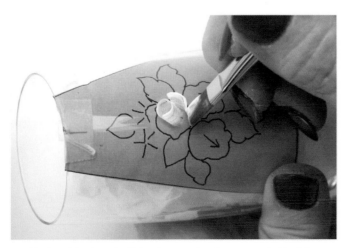

3 Re-load the brush. Paint the petal to the upper right of the cup with a comma stroke. The paint corner of the brush is always at the outside edge of the petal.

4 Re-load and paint the petal to the upper left of the cup with a comma stroke. Turn the glass so it is in a comfortable painting position to pull the stroke.

roses, leaves and filler flowers

5 Re-load and paint the lower right petal.

6 Re-load and paint the lower left petal.

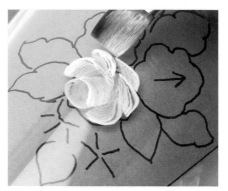

7 Re-load and paint the bottom petal left to right.

8 Paint the other two roses the same way, facing them in the direction of the arrows shown on the pattern.

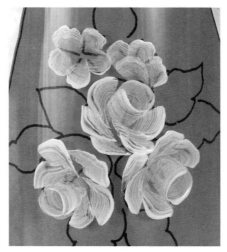

9 To paint the five-petal filler flowers at the top of the design, use a no. 4 shader. Paint the open flower first, then the tipped one. The open flower is a series of five open-crescent strokes (see page 15 for this stroke technique). The tipped flower is three open-crescent strokes. The bottom petal is a comma stroke with the paint corner of the brush facing the top edge of the petal.

10 To paint the leaves, load a no. 6 shader as described in Step 1 on page 39. Keeping the paint corner of the brush to the outside edge of the leaf, start at the base of the leaf and pull toward the tip.

11 Flip your brush over so the paint corner of the brush is to the outside edge, and immediately paint the other half of the leaf.

12 Finish painting the leaves, working outward on the design. Thin the pearl white mix with a little Flow Medium and use a 10/0 liner to add the center vein in each leaf.

13 This floral design is repeated two more times on the glass. Use the same pattern and the positioning template shown on page 38 to place them evenly around the glass. Paint them just as you did the first one. After all the floral designs on the glass are painted, remove the pattern from inside the glass, and remove any tape residue and registration marks. Place a crumpled piece of dark-colored tissue inside the glass so you can see your strokes. The ribbons that link all three floral designs are painted freehand. Work a speck of Clear Medium into the no. 4 shader by blending on the palette. Load the brush in the pearl white mix and start the ribbon by painting an S-stroke.

14 Come from the other direction with another S-stroke to join the ribbon. Complete all the ribbons on the glass the same way.

15 Thin the pearl white mix with Flow Medium. Use a fine stylus to dot on the pollen dots on the filler flowers and the dots along the edges of the ribbons all around the glass. Hold the glass by the stem so you do not smudge your dots. Let these dots dry completely before handling the glass again.

16 Repeat these instructions for the second glass. You will need two crystal flutes—one for the bride and one for the groom—to use for toasting during the wedding reception.

reverse-painted
fruit plates

materials

PAINTS
Autumn Leaves
Burnt Sienna
Burnt Umber
Butter Pecan
Engine Red
Hunter Green
Italian Sage
Lemon Custard
Licorice
Pure Orange
School Bus Yellow
Sunflower
Warm White
Yellow Ochre

BRUSHES
no. 6 scumbler
nos. 6 and 8 shaders
no. 2 round

SURFACES
Clear glass dessert plates,
8 inches (20.3cm) in diameter,
by Luminarc/Arcoroc Cristelle,
#8064084, available from
www.villagekitchen.com.
Similar glass plates available at
home centers and craft stores.

ADDITIONAL SUPPLIES
Craft knife
Fine stylus
FolkArt Blank Adhesive Stencil
#4167

This is traditional reverse painting on
glass. The design is painted on the back side of the plate in
reverse order: the highlights first, then the shading layers and
finally the basecoat. A stippling technique gives a more interesting and realistic texture to the fruit.

COLORS

Italian Sage

Pure Orange

School Bus Yellow

Sunflower

Warm White

Yellow Ochre

COLOR MIXES

BRIGHT YELLOW MIX:
School Bus Yellow +
Lemon Custard 1:1

LIGHT YELLOW MIX:
Warm White + a touch
of Bright Yellow mix

**GOLDEN BROWN
MIX:**
Yellow Ochre + Burnt
Sienna 3:1

REDDISH BROWN MIX:
Autumn Leaves + Burnt
Sienna 1:1 + a touch of
Engine Red

LIGHT BROWN MIX:
Butter Pecan + Burnt
Sienna 2:1

DARK BROWN MIX:
Burnt Umber + a touch
of Licorice

DARK GREEN MIX:
Hunter Green + Burnt
Sienna 1: 1½

**MEDIUM GREEN
MIX:**
Dark Green Mix +
Italian Sage 1:1

DARK YELLOW MIX:
Yellow Ochre + a touch
of Burnt Sienna

**WARM YELLOW
MIX:**
Sunflower + Warm
White 1:1

WARM RED MIX:
Engine Red + Pure
Orange 1:1

DARK RED MIX:
Warm Red Mix + a
touch of Burnt Sienna

**GOLDEN YELLOW
MIX:**
Yellow Ochre + a touch
of Sunflower

patterns

Pears

These patterns may be hand-traced or photocopied for personal use only. Enlarge them at 200%, then again at 106% to bring them up to full size.

Apples

1 Clean the back of the plate with alcohol and a soft cloth. Tape the pattern face down on the front so you can see it from the back through the bottom of the glass plate.

2 Transfer just the pear shapes from the pattern to a sheet of blank adhesive stencil and cut them out with a craft knife.

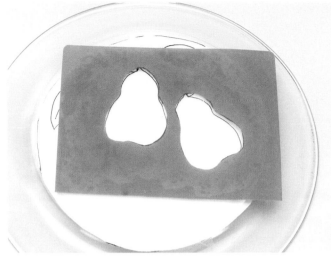

3 Peel off the protective backing and place the stencil on the back of the plate, following the pattern, and press the edges down so there's no paint seepage.

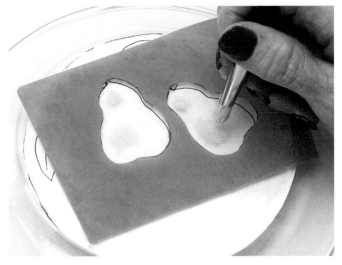

4 Mix 1 part School Bus Yellow and 1 part Lemon Custard to make a bright yellow. Mix a touch of the bright yellow into a puddle of Warm White to make a light yellow. Using a no. 6 scumbler brush, tap into the puddle of light yellow and offload excess paint onto a dry paper towel. Tap on the brightest highlight on your pears at the top left and lower left (as you look at them through the back of the plate). Wipe this color off the brush onto a paper towel. Do not clean your brush in water between loads.

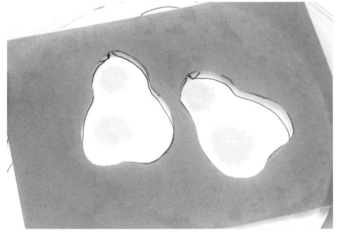

5 To make the second highlight, tap over the first highlight with the bright yellow mix, starting in the center of the first highlight and enlarging it. Always offload excess paint onto a paper towel after you re-load.

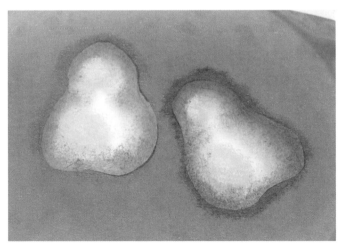

6 To shade the pears, mix 3 parts Yellow Ochre and 1 part Burnt Sienna to make a golden brown. Mix equal parts of Autumn Leaves and Burnt Sienna plus a touch of Engine Red to make a reddish brown. Start on the left pear and tap on the golden brown to shade it along the lower half and up the right side of the pear. Where the pear indents in the middle, pull the shading in toward the center. Continue up and over the top and down the left. Shade the right pear the same way using the reddish-brown mix first, then shade over that with the golden brown mix. Wipe your brush off on a paper towel between loads.

pear plate

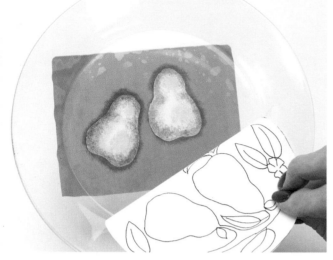

7 Untape one side of the pattern and check your work. This is how your plate looks now from the front.

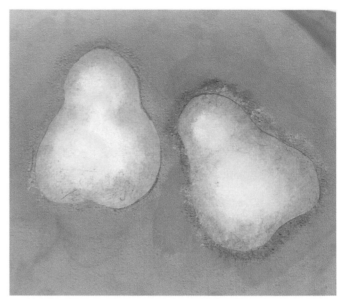

8 Turn your plate over to the back again and stipple a lacy coat of School Bus Yellow over the entire area of both pears. Let dry.

9 Stipple a solid coat of Yellow Ochre over the entire area of both pears, starting in the center and working out toward the edges of the stencil.

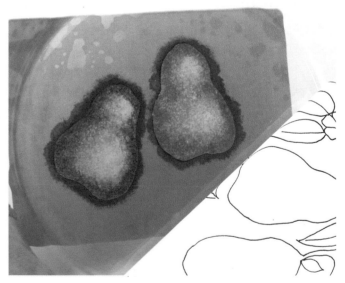

10 Untape one side of the pattern. This is how the finished pears look from the front. Pull the green stencil off before the paint dries and then let the paint dry completely so you don't smudge it while you're working on the leaves and branches. Re-tape the pattern back in place on the front of the plate before continuing.

BRANCHES

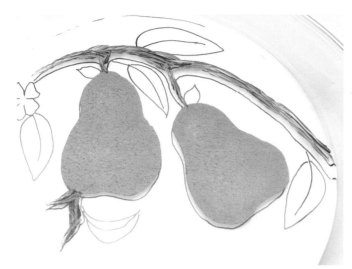

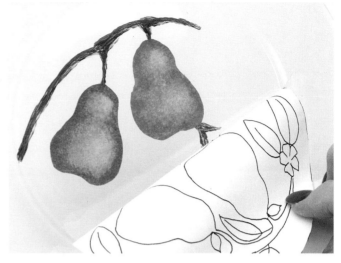

11 Mix 2 parts Butter Pecan and 1 part Burnt Sienna to make a light brown. Mix Burnt Umber and a touch of Licorice to make a dark brown. Using a no. 8 shader, load one flat side in the light brown and the other flat side in the dark brown. Begin the branches and stems with short choppy strokes, staying up on the chisel edge and always keeping the dark brown side of the brush toward the fruit. Let dry.

12 Apply another coat to the branches, using the same choppy strokes to get a rough, bark-like texture.

LEAVES

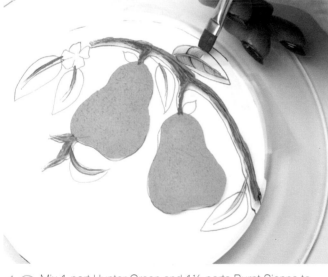

13 Mix 1 part Hunter Green and 1½ parts Burnt Sienna to make a dark green. Mix equal parts of this dark green with Italian Sage to make a medium green. Use a no. 8 shader and load one flat side into the dark green and the other flat side into medium green. Staying up on the chisel edge, draw in the center vein on each leaf. To paint the leaves, keep the dark green side of the brush toward the glass and pull individual segments out from the vein, starting at the base and working toward the tip.

14 Finish all the leaves, including the small single-stroke leaves which are painted with a no. 6 shader. Let dry.

15 Top-coat the leaves with either Italian Sage + a drop of Flow Medium, or Sunflower + a drop of Flow Medium, to vary the colors and add interest. These top coats are just brushed on; you do not need to repaint each segment of the leaf.

pear blossoms

16 Since these are reverse painted, start with the green pollen dots. Dot them on with the fine stylus and the dark green mix.

17 Use a no. 2 round to stipple right over the green pollen dots with School Bus Yellow. To begin the pear blossom petals, mix a dark yellow using Yellow Ochre and a touch of Burnt Sienna; mix a warm yellow with equal parts Sunflower and Warm White. Using a no. 6 shader, load one flat side of the brush into the dark yellow; load the other flat side into light yellow. With the light yellow side toward the glass, pull three petals in a Y-shape. Re-load for each petal.

18 Pull the other two petals to complete the pear blossom.

19 Add a few pear blossoms to the rim of the plate if you wish. The leaves on either side are single-stroke leaves using the dark and medium green mixes and a no. 6 shader.

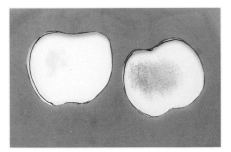

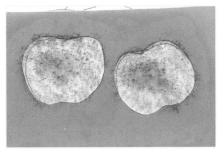

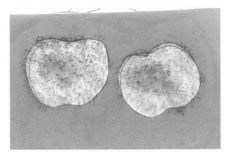

20 To stipple the apples, start with the lightest highlights on the upper left of both apples with Warm White. Offload most of the paint on your scumbler brush onto a dry paper towel so the highlight is very subtle. The second highlight of Pure Orange is stippled over the first highlight and extended into the center of the apple.

21 Mix equal parts Engine Red and Pure Orange on your palette. Stipple a lacy coat of this warm red mix over the entire area of both apples.

22 To the warm red mix, add a touch of Burnt Sienna to make a dark red. Shade the apples, widest along the bottom and up the right side. The shading should be more opaque along the edges and lacier as you go toward the center (feather the edges of the shading as you stipple in the center). Let dry.

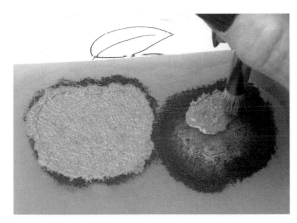

23 Stipple a solid coat of Yellow Ochre over both apples, starting in the centers and working outward.

24 This is how the finished apples look from the front. Carefully remove the stencil while the paint is still wet, and let dry completely.

25 The apple blossom petals are painted the same way as the pear blossoms. Use the dark red mix from Step 22 above; mix a golden yellow with Yellow Ochre + a touch of Sunflower. Use a no. 6 shader and keep the golden yellow side toward the glass as you paint each apple blossom. The leaves on either side are single-stroke leaves using the dark and medium green mixes from Step 13 and a no. 6 shader. Let dry completely.

vintage
red goblets

materials

PAINTS

Burnt Sienna
Metallic Gold
Yellow Ochre

BRUSHES

no. 6 shader
JS 10/0 liner
nos. 2 and 4 filberts

SURFACES

Red glass goblets with clear
glass stems and base, found
at a flea market. Similar
goblets can be found at home
stores and gift shops.

ADDITIONAL SUPPLIES

Fine stylus
Clear Medium
Flow Medium

These lovely crimson-colored goblets
were found at a local flea market and needed only a bit of color
to enhance their beauty. The color palette of Burnt Sienna,
Yellow Ochre and Metallic Gold adds an understated elegance
that would be perfect in a traditional setting. I found red cloth
napkins edged with gold thread at my local store and painted a
matching roses-and-leaves design on one corner using regular
acrylic paints. Adapt this design to any red water goblets or wine
glasses and you'll have something special for your own holiday
dinner table!

COLORS

Burnt Sienna   Metallic Gold

COLOR MIXES

MIX A: MIX B:
Yellow Ochre + Burnt Yellow Ochre +
Sienna 3:1   Mix A 1:1

pattern

This pattern may be hand-traced or photocopied for personal use only. Enlarge at 145% to bring it up to full size. Cut out the pattern and cut along the vertical "release lines." Place the pattern inside the goblet, taping it securely in place.

PAINT THE ROSE PETALS IN THIS ORDER

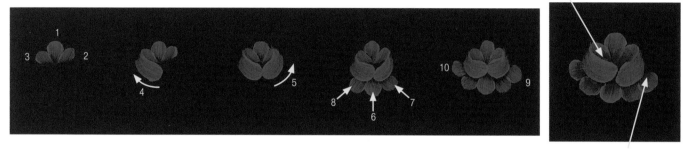

Shade

Sideload float Burnt Sienna

1 The roses are all painted with the same colors, built up layer by layer. Layer 1: Begin with the no. 4 filbert and Burnt Sienna. Paint the first color layer on the rose petals and the buds. Thin Burnt Sienna with Flow Medium and use a 10/0 liner for the stems.

2 Layer 2: Mix 3 parts Yellow Ochre and 1 part Burnt Sienna to make "Mix A." Load Burnt Sienna on one flat side of the no. 4 filbert, and Mix A on the other flat side. Keeping the Burnt Sienna side toward the glass, paint layer 2 over Layer 1. Let dry.

3 Layer 3: Mix 1 part Yellow Ochre with 1 part of the Mix A you used for Layer 2. This new mix is called "Mix B." On no. 4 filbert, load one flat side in Mix A and the other side in Mix B. With the Mix A side toward the glass, paint this new layer over the previous 2 layers on the rose and the buds. Paint the small leaves with the chisel edge of a no. 2 filbert, one flat side loaded in Burnt Sienna, the other side loaded in Mix B.

4 Shading: Double load a no. 6 shader in Clear Medium and Burnt Sienna and blend on your palette. Shade each rose inside the cup and along the base of the cup; shade the base of the petals and the buds.

5 Highlights: Load one flat side of a no. 4 filbert in Mix B and the other flat side in Metallic Gold. Highlight the three back petals of the rose, the 5 small lower petals, and the widest end of the buds. Do a traditional double-load on a no. 4 filbert using Mix A and Metallic Gold. Blend slightly on the palette. Highlight the two large side petals, with the Gold side of the brush toward the top of the rose. Load one flat side of a no. 2 filbert in Clear Medium and the other side in Metallic Gold and use the chisel edge to highlight each small leaf.

6 Dip Dots: Add a few drops of Flow Medium to Mix B and use a fine stylus to add pollen dots inside the cup of the rose and below the buds. Refer to the pattern for placement.

red cloth napkin

The napkin is painted with acrylics; textile medium is added to the paints and also used as a floating medium. Refer to the goblet instructions for techniques and brush sizes. Use pins and tape to mount the laundered napkin onto plastic-covered cardboard. Undercoat the design with textile medium + Warm White (2:1) and when dry, basecoat with textile medium + Yellow Ochre (2:1). Shade flowers and buds with Burnt Sienna; highlight with Yellow Ochre + touch of Warm White. Use this same yellow mix for the pollen dots. Add metallic highlights with a sideload float of Inca Gold + Metallic Gold (2:1).

trumpet flower
tea lights

materials

PAINTS

Autumn Leaves
Engine Red
Fresh Foliage
Italian Sage
Licorice
Pure Orange
School Bus Yellow
Skin Tone
Sunflower
Thicket
Warm White
Yellow Ochre

BRUSHES

no. 4 shader
no. 1 liner
no. 4 filbert

SURFACES

Hanging glass candle holders,
"Squirly," 2½-inches (6.4 cm)
square and 5 inches (12.7 cm)
tall, available online from Crate
& Barrel.

ADDITIONAL SUPPLIES

Fine stylus
Clear Medium
Flow Medium

Unique glass lanterns, three brushes

and some bright color mixes combine to create these charming tea lights for your patio or an outdoor party. Paint all three
in your favorite color or paint the three different color versions
shown here. Use tea light candles in clear plastic holders so the
lanterns look delicate. If you want to hang these lanterns from
tree branches, use strong fishing line and tie them up out of the
way—they will look as if they are floating on air.

COLORS

School Bus Yellow   Autumn Leaves   Yellow Ochre

COLOR MIXES

WARM RED MIX:
Engine Red + Pure
Orange 2:1

PINK MIX:
Engine Red + Skin
Tone 1:1

DARK GREEN MIX:
Thicket + speck of
Licorice

LIGHT GREEN MIX:
Italian Sage + Fresh
Foliage + 2:1

PALE PEACH MIX:
Warm White + Skin
Tone 4:1

PALE YELLOW MIX:
Warm White +
Sunflower 3:1

**BRIGHT
ORANGE MIX:**
Pure Orange + School
Bus Yellow 1:1

patterns

Full side

Half side

These patterns may be hand-traced or photocopied for personal use only. Enlarge them at 127% to bring them up to full size.

1 Place the patterns inside the glass lantern and add crumpled tissue or paper towels to hold the patterns up against the glass.

2 Mix 2 parts Engine Red + 1 part Pure Orange on your palette for a warm red. In another area, mix equal parts Engine Red and Skin Tone for a pink. Using a no. 4 filbert, load one flat side in the pink mix and the other flat side in the red mix. Use the chisel edge and make a long narrow stroke for the base of each trumpet flower. The buds are shorter strokes of the same colors. Re-load for each stroke.

4 For the pollen dots, thin School Bus Yellow with Flow Medium. Use a fine stylus to dot on four or five dots in the center of the four-petal flowers.

3 The petals at the top of each flower where the trumpet flares out and opens up are painted with the same brush and colors using a "touch-pause-pull" stroke. Touch the brush to the surface, pause to let the bristles flare out a little, then finish with a quick pull of the brush. Do this four times for each flower. For the top center petal and the right petal, keep the pink side of the brush toward the glass. Re-load, and paint the left petal with the pink side toward the glass. Flip the brush over so the red side is toward the glass and paint the bottom petal left to right.

5 Mix Thicket + a speck of Licorice + Flow Medium to make a dark green. Prepare a light green mix from 2 parts Italian Sage + 1 part Fresh Foliage + Flow Medium. Double load a no. 1 liner and start at the top of the glass lantern. Pull the vines downward following the pattern lines. Re-load for each stroke, and touch the loaded brush to the palette to remove excess paint. These strokes should be more sheer than opaque—you want the candlelight to shine through the paint.

red trumpet flowers

6 Remove the pattern pieces from inside the glass lantern and check that all the flowers and buds are connected to a vine. The leaves will be painted freehand; refer to the pattern for placement. Mix Thicket + a speck of Licorice for a dark green; mix 2 parts Italian Sage + 1 part Fresh Foliage for a light green. (Flow Medium is not added to these green mixes.) You'll be using these two greens for the sepals on the base of each trumpet flower and bud, plus all the leaves. Double load the no. 1 liner and paint the sepals starting at the base of the trumpet and pulling up along the base, then wiggle outward.

7 Double load a no. 4 shader and paint the single-stroke leaves, following the leaf placement on the pattern. You can paint three leaves before you'll need to re-load the brush. Let dry completely.

orange and yellow trumpet flowers

ORANGE TRUMPET FLOWERS

The orange trumpet flowers and buds are painted the same way as the red flowers in steps 1-7, using the following color mix for the flowers: Pale peach mix = 4 parts Warm White + 1 part Skin Tone. Load one flat side of the no. 4 filbert in the pale peach mix and the other flat side in Autumn Leaves. Use the chisel edge and make a long narrow stroke for the base of each trumpet flower. The buds are shorter strokes of the same colors. Re-load between each stroke. The petals at the top of each flower where the trumpet flares out and opens up are painted with the same brush and colors using a "touch-pause-pull" stroke. Touch the brush to the surface, pause to let the bristles flare out a little, then finish with a quick pull of the brush. Do this four times for each flower. For the top center petal and the right petal, keep the pale peach side of the brush toward the glass. Re-load, and paint the left petal with the pale peach side toward the glass. Flip the brush over so the Autumn Leaves side is toward the glass and paint the bottom petal left to right. Paint all the orange trumpet flowers the same way. Follow steps 4-7 on pages 57-58 using the same brushes and colors to paint the pollen dots, vines, sepals and leaves.

YELLOW TRUMPET FLOWERS

The yellow trumpet flowers and buds are painted the same way as the red flowers in steps 1-7, using the following color mix for the flowers: Pale yellow mix = 3 parts Warm White + 1 part Sunflower. Load one flat side of the no. 4 filbert in the pale yellow mix and the other flat side in Yellow Ochre. Use the chisel edge and make a long narrow stroke for the base of each trumpet flower. The buds are shorter strokes of the same colors. Re-load between each stroke. The petals at the top of each flower where the trumpet flares out and opens up are painted with the same brush and colors using a "touch-pause-pull" stroke. Touch the brush to the surface, pause to let the bristles flare out a little, then finish with a quick pull of the brush. Do this four times for each flower. For the top center petal and the right petal, keep the pale yellow side of the brush toward the glass. Re-load, and paint the left petal with the pale yellow side toward the glass. Flip the brush over so the Yellow Ochre side is toward the glass and paint the bottom petal left to right. Paint all the yellow trumpet flowers the same way. For the pollen dots, use a fine stylus and a bright orange mix of equal parts Pure Orange and School Bus Yellow + a touch of Clear Medium. Add four or five dots in the center of the four-petal flowers. Follow steps 5-7 on pages 57-58 using the same brushes and colors to paint the vines, sepals and leaves.

crystal decanter &
cordial glasses

materials

PAINTS
Burnt Sienna
Metallic Gold

BRUSHES
JS no. 1 liner

SURFACES
Round crystal decanter by
Mikasa, and stemmed 3¼-oz.
"Grappa" cordial glasses by
Spiegelau.

ADDITIONAL SUPPLIES
Stylus
Flow Medium
Scissors

The combination of Burnt Sienna and Metallic

Gold give the traditional strokework on this crystal decanter and
cordial glasses a rich coppery glow. A pattern is placed inside
the cordial glasses, but the decanter is painted freehand without
a pattern. The design is really just a combination of simple
comma strokes, so do give it a try. Any errant strokes can be
easily removed with a bit of rubbing alcohol and a cotton swab
or wooden skewer.

COLORS

Burnt Sienna   Metallic Gold

patterns

Decanter top

Cordial glass

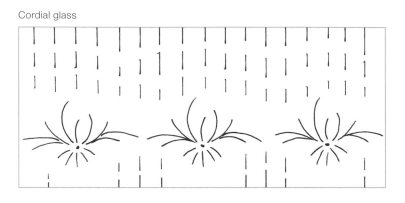

Decanter side

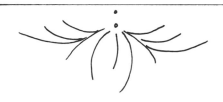

These patterns may be hand-traced or photocopied for personal use only. Enlarge the Decanter Top and Side patterns at 110%. Enlarge the Cordial Glass pattern at 141%. The Cordial Glass Base pattern is shown at 100%.

Base of cordial glass

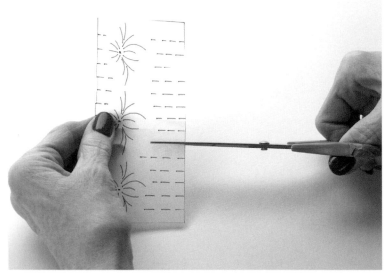

2 Insert the pattern inside the glass, press it into place and tape it at a couple of places along the top rim.

1 Trace and transfer the pattern to plain white bond paper. Prepare the cordial glass for painting by taping the base pattern to the bottom of the stemmed glass. For the main design on the glass, make release cuts along the broken lines on the pattern. Tape the two ends together to form a cylinder.

3 Thin the two colors, Metallic Gold and Burnt Sienna, with a few drops of Flow Medium. Load a no. 1 JS liner in Burnt Sienna, tip into the Metallic Gold, touch the tip to your palette to blend the paints. Paint comma strokes following the pattern. Re-load for each stroke. After each stroke, wipe off the brush lightly on a soft paper towel. Paint the base with the same colors and brush, following the pattern. The center dot is made with a stylus. Dot on the Burnt Sienna first, let it dry, then dot on the Metallic Gold with the smaller end of the stylus.

4 On the decanter, the design is painted free-hand following the pattern for the base of the glass. The design repeats five times around the decanter where it flares out and then becomes straight-sided. Use the same brush and colors as used for the cordial glass. Begin with the bottom half of the design. Turn the decanter upside down and hold it by the neck to make painting easier. The two halves are a mirror image.

5 Finish with the top half of the design. Let dry completely.

pink geranium coaster &
goblet set

materials

PAINTS
Baby Pink
Engine Red
Italian Sage
Lemon Custard
Licorice
Pure Orange
Thicket

BRUSHES
nos. 4 and 6 filberts
no. 2 round
JS 10/0 and no. 1 liners

SURFACES
16-ounce clear glass goblets,
7 inches (17.8cm) tall, 3-inch
(7.6cm) diameter top, available
at home centers and department stores.

ADDITIONAL SUPPLIES
Flow Medium
18 kt. Gold Leafing Pen
Scissors

Bring a bit of summer right to the table with these bright pink geraniums painted on clear glass water goblets. Use filbert brushes to make quick work of painting the variegated petals and leaves. Paint a few geraniums on a glass pitcher and you'll have the perfect set for serving those cool summertime beverages. The coordinating coasters are painted on Kreative Kanvas, a sturdy synthetic canvas, using regular acrylic paints.

COLOR MIXES

WARM RED MIX:
Engine Red + Pure
Orange 4:1

PINK MIX:
Baby Pink + a touch of
Warm Red mix

DARK GREEN MIX:
Thicket + a speck of
Licorice

**YELLOW-GREEN
MIX:**
Lemon Custard +
Italian Sage 2:1

patterns

Goblet

PREPARATION

Trace and transfer the goblet pattern to a sheet of white bond paper. Cut out the pattern along the solid outline, then make "release cuts" along the broken lines. Butt the short edges together to form a cylinder with the pattern to the outside and tape the ends together. Position the pattern inside the glass, aligning the top of the pattern to the top of the glass (see Step 1 photo at top of next page). Tape the pattern in place. Slightly moisten your fingertips and "mold" the pattern against the inside surface of the glass. Use the handle of a plastic palette knife if you cannot reach the bottom of the pattern with your fingers.

This pattern may be hand-traced or photocopied for personal use only. Enlarge at 143% to bring it up to full size.

Coaster

This pattern may be hand-traced or photocopied for personal use only. Enlarge at 139% to bring it up to full size. Transfer the pattern to a small piece of sturdy synthetic canvas. Paint the coaster following the instructions on page 69.

1 To paint the florets of the geranium blossom, mix 4 parts Engine Red and 1 part Pure Orange to make a warm red. Mix a touch of the red mix into a puddle of Baby Pink to make a pink mix. Using a no. 6 filbert, load one flat side into the pink and the other flat side into the red. With the pink side of the brush toward the glass, paint the top petal and the two side petals. Flip the brush over so the red side is toward the glass and paint the bottom petal left to right to complete the floret. Occasionally wipe your brush lightly on a paper towel between re-loads.

2 Continue adding more four-petal florets, varying them in size by the pressure on your brush. Angle the florets along the sides so they're not all facing upward.

3 Finish filling in the geranium blossom, following the pattern. Add a few random strokes with the chisel edge of the brush along the outside edge.

4 Load a no. 4 filbert in the red and pink mixes as you did in Step 1 and paint the unopened buds below the main blossom using the chisel edge of the brush.

centers, stems and leaves

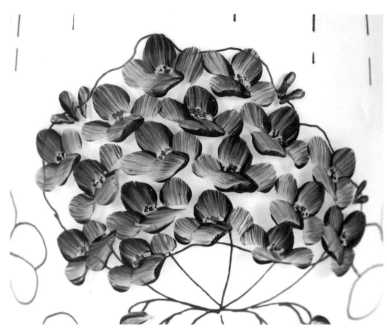

5 Mix Thicket + a speck of Licorice for a dark green. Mix 2 parts Lemon Custard + 1 part Italian Sage for a yellow-green. Mix in a few drops of Flow Medium to each green mix. With a no. 2 round, stipple in the centers first with the yellow-green mix. Then stipple on tiny dots of dark green.

6 Load a no. 1 liner in the dark green mix and paint all the stems supporting the bottom of the geranium blossom, extending a few stems upward in and among the florets. Also paint the stems for the unopened buds, and the stems of the green leaves. Double load a no. 1 liner in dark green on one side and yellow-green on the other. Paint a tiny stroke on either side of the buds for the sepals.

7 Begin painting the leaves with the same dark and yellow-green mixes, but without Flow Medium this time. Use a no. 6 filbert and load yellow-green on one flat side and dark green on the other. With the yellow-green toward the glass surface, stroke each lobe of the leaf, puling downward toward the top of the stem. Start with the center lobe, then the right side, then the left, alternating sides. Finish all the leaves with these green mixes and let them dry completely before continuing.

8 To detail the leaves, use a 10/0 liner and the warm red mix thinned with Flow Medium. Pull each fine line from the center outward on each leaf lobe, following the shape of the lobe.

Finished gera-
nium goblets

canvas coaster

Paint coordinating coasters using regular acrylic
paints and a sturdy synthetic canvas cut to shape
(see page 126 for resources). Unless otherwise spec-
ified, use the same color mixes as for the goblets.
For each coaster, basecoat both sides of a 5½-inch
(14cm) square piece of Kreative Kanvas with a pale
green mix of Warm White + Lemon Custard + Italian
Sage (2:1:1). Let dry. Transfer the coaster pattern
on page 66 to the basecoated surface. Add a speck
of Licorice to the red mix and paint the first layer of
florets. Paint a second layer of florets randomly over
the first layer using the goblet colors; paint the buds.
Stipple on the flower centers. Paint the stems and
sepals with Thicket; shade with the dark green mix.
Paint the leaves and add the fine red linework. Erase
any visible tracing lines. Apply two coats of brush-on
matte varnish to each side of the coaster. When dry,
use scissors to cut out the coasters along the pattern
lines. Apply gold to the cut edge with a Gold Leafing
Pen. Let dry thoroughly before handling.

spanish folk art
condiment set

PAINTS

Autumn Leaves

Periwinkle

Yellow Ochre

Italian Sage

Thicket

BRUSHES

10/0 script liner

no. 2 round

JS no. 1 liner

no. 1 liner

nos. 2, 6 and 8 shaders

SURFACES

Tray: White porcelain platter, 19½ inches x 6¾ inches (49.5 cm x 17.1 cm), available online from Crate & Barrel.

Vinegar & Oil Cruets: White porcelain 8-ounce bottles with metal tips, available at Pottery Barn.

Salt & Pepper Shakers: White china shakers, "Great White," available at Pottery Barn.

ADDITIONAL SUPPLIES

Flow Medium

Extender

¼-inch (6mm) masking tape

Flexible measuring tape

Fine stylus

Blue china marker

Sharpie Ultra Fine Point pen

The strokework designs on this condiment set

are in the warm colors of the Mediterranean and were inspired by the folk art pottery I've seen on my trips to Spain. At first glance, the designs may seem rather complex, but look closely and you'll recognize the basic leaf strokes, "S" strokes, comma strokes and crescent strokes. Simple techniques for striping and design layout, along with a limited palette, make this an especially enjoyable painting project. Put together a set of white china salt and pepper shakers, vinegar and oil cruets, and a tray to hold them and they'll look great on your kitchen table!

COLORS

Periwinkle   Yellow Ochre   Autumn Leaves

COLOR MIXES

GREEN MIX:
Italian Sage +
Thicket 2:1

tray

PREPARATION

Flow Medium is added to thin the paint (unless otherwise instructed) to achieve a translucent, almost rustic effect. A pattern is not used for any of these pieces; instead use a flexible measuring tape and a marker to mark where to place dip dots, from which the designs on the cruets and salt & pepper shakers develop.

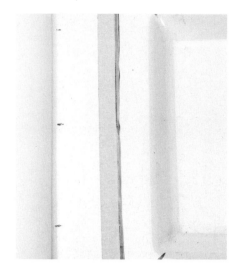

1. Begin with the short sides of the tray. Use ¼-inch (6mm) masking tape and tape off ½-inch (13mm) in on the rim for the checkerboard pattern. Miter the tape at the corners. Burnish the tape down well to prevent paint seepage. Use a china marker to place a hash mark at the center of the tray 3½ inches (8.9 cm) from either edge. Then place a hash mark on the edge of the tray every 1½ inches (3.8 cm) using the china marker. You should have a total of three hash marks along the short side of the tray. Mix equal parts Periwinkle and Extender. Use a JS no. 1 liner to paint the blue stripe. Remove the tape before the paint begins to dry.

2. Thin Periwinkle with a little Flow Medium and use a number 6 shader to paint the checkerboard pattern, starting in the middle under the center hash mark. Paint the checks all the way to the corner.

3. Finish the checkerboard to the other corner. Thin Yellow Ochre with Flow Medium and use a no. 8 shader to paint a two-stroke leaf with a small S-stroke on each side. Paint three leaves across the short end of the tray (this may vary depending on the size and shape of your tray). Space them evenly, using the hash marks to guide your placement.

4. Thin Autumn Leaves with a little Flow Medium and use the 10/0 liner to paint three red comma strokes on the yellow leaves. Finish with two elongated comma strokes on each side of the S-strokes using the 10/0 liner and a green mix of 2 parts Italian Sage + 1 part Thicket, thinned with Flow Medium. Remove the hash marks with a dry cloth and let the paint dry completely.

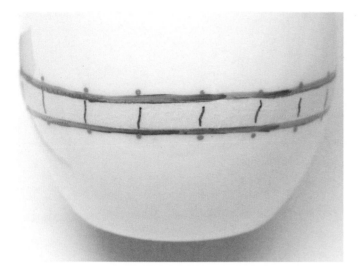

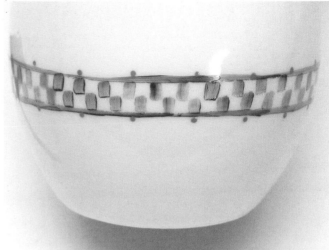

1 Use a flexible tape measure and a china marker to place hash marks just above 1½ inches (3.8 cm) from the bottom of the cruet. Apply the ¼-inch (6 mm) masking tape around the cruet just below the marks. Use a dry cotton swab to remove the hash marks and clean the area with a paper towel barely moistened with rubbing alcohol. Burnish the masking tape well to prevent paint seepage. At every ½ inch (13 mm) put a line across the tape with an ultra-fine point black marker. Adjust the last few marks if the measurement doesn't come out to be exact. Mix equal parts Periwinkle and Extender and paint a line above and below the tape using a JS no. 1 liner. Hold your brush steady in one hand and rotate the cruet bottle with your other hand. Above and below the tape, use a very fine stylus to place a tiny dip dot of Yellow Ochre at each mark on the tape. Remove the tape quickly before the paint dries.

2 Thin Periwinkle with a few drops of Flow Medium and use a no. 2 shader to paint a checkerboard pattern between the two blue lines. Adjust your checkerboard near the end if it isn't coming out quite evenly.

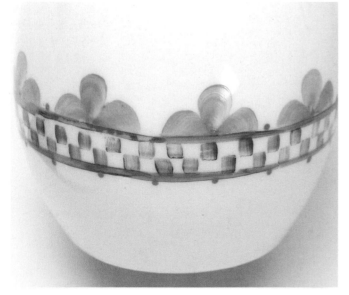

3 Paint the half-flowers with thinned Yellow Ochre on a no. 6 shader. Paint a closed-crescent stroke for the middle petal and add a half-crescent on each side.

4 With Autumn Leaves thinned with Flow Medium on a no. 6 shader, tap thin vein lines on the petals using the chisel edge of the brush.

vinegar & oil cruets

5 With the same green mix you used on the tray (see step 4 on page 72) and a JS no. 1 liner, paint a short comma stroke above each side petal of the yellow half-flowers, then a long comma stroke that begins above the center petal. Use a fine stylus and thinned Autumn Leaves for the four dip-dots.

6 Load thinned Autumn Leaves on a no. 2 round to paint the red flowers. Paint the center stroke; re-load and paint two shorter strokes on each side. The blue comma strokes are done with the JS no. 1 liner and thinned Periwinkle.

8 If desired, add part of the design from the salt & pepper shakers to the neck of the cruet, adjusting for the narrower neck of the bottle. Paint the blue checkerboard, then follow Steps 4 and 5 on the next page for the rest of the design.

7 Repeat the yellow half-flowers and blue comma strokes below the checkerboard, offsetting them from the ones above. Let dry completely.

1 Use a flexible tape measure and a china marker to place hash marks just above 1½ inches (3.8 cm) from the bottom of the shaker. Apply the ¼-inch (6 mm) masking tape around the shaker just below the marks. Use a dry cotton swab to remove the hash marks and clean the area with a paper towel barely moistened with rubbing alcohol. Burnish the masking tape well to prevent paint seepage. At every ½ inch (13 mm) put a line across the tape with a fine point black marker. Adjust the last few marks if the measurement doesn't come out to be exact. Mix equal parts Periwinkle and Extender and paint a line above and below the tape using a JS no. 1 liner. Hold your brush steady in one hand and rotate the shaker using your other hand. Above and below the tape, use a very fine stylus to place a tiny dip dot of Yellow Ochre at each mark on the tape. Remove the tape quickly before the paint dries. Thin Periwinkle with a few drops of Flow Medium and use a no. 2 shader to paint a checkerboard pattern between the two blue lines. Adjust your checkerboard near the end if it isn't coming out quite evenly. Paint red five-stroke flowers above each yellow dip dot using a no. 2 round and thinned Autumn Leaves.

2 Touch on tiny leaves at the base of the red flowers with the green mix (2 parts Italian Sage + 1 part Thicket, thinned with Flow Medium) on a no. 2 round.

3 Add Yellow Ochre dip-dots above the flowers with a fine stylus. Use the JS liner to pull two comma strokes with the green mix.

4 Use a no. 1 liner and thinned Periwinkle and paint the two blue comma strokes along the top of the design. Load a no. 2 round in thinned Yellow Ochre; add a tiny stroke between the two blue commas, and a small stroke below. Below the checkerboard, use thinned Yellow Ochre and the no. 6 shader to paint the two-stroke leaf between each set of dip dots.

5 Work a little Extender into the no. 6 shader and pick up undiluted Autumn Leaves on the corner for a sideload float. Shade the yellow leaves where they meet the blue stripe. Load a 10/0 liner in thinned Autumn Leaves and paint three red comma strokes over the yellow leaf shapes. Between the leaves, add three comma strokes and a dot with thinned Periwinkle. Let dry completely.

oak leaves on
candle holder

materials

PAINTS

Burnt Sienna

Burnt Umber

Butter Pecan

Yellow Ochre

BRUSH

no. 8 shader

nos. 6 and 8 filberts

JS 10/0 and no. 1 liners

SURFACES

Clear glass pillar candle holder with black wood stand by Horizon, available at Bed Bath & Beyond

ADDITIONAL SUPPLIES

Clear Medium

Flow Medium

This large glass candle holder and black wooden base have a bold, masculine look that would be perfect in a rustic setting or if you are aiming for that "lodge" look. The stylized oak leaves and acorns were inspired by a gilt border that I admired on an antique museum-piece table. I limited the palette to a few shades of brown to keep things simple. Adding the acorn and leaf design to the wooden base would make this a unique and handsome gift for a man.

COLORS

Burnt Umber

COLOR MIXES

LIGHT BROWN MIX:
Butter Pecan + Burnt Umber + Yellow Ochre 4:3:1

DARK BROWN MIX:
Burnt Sienna + Burnt Umber 1:1

pattern

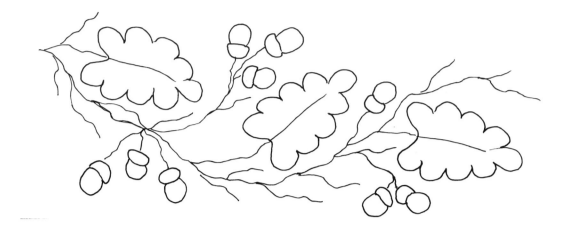

This pattern may be hand-traced or photocopied for personal use only. Enlarge at 130% to bring it up to full size.

OAK LEAVES

1 Tape the pattern to the inside of the glass candle holder. Mix 4 parts Butter Pecan, 3 parts Burnt Umber, and 1 part Yellow Ochre to make a light brown mix. For the dark brown, mix equal parts Burnt Sienna and Burnt Umber. Load one flat side of a no. 8 filbert in the light brown mix, the other flat side in the dark brown mix. With the light brown side of the brush toward the glass, pull a single stroke for the top lobe of the oak leaf.

2 Continue with the next two lobes of the leaf. Use enough pressure on the filbert to create a defining edge on each lobe.

3 Finish the oak leaf with six more side-by-side lobes. Paint the rest of the leaves around the candle holder the same way. Let dry.

ACORNS

4 Switch to a no. 6 filbert and load it the same way and with the same colors as for the leaves. To paint the body of the acorn, pull a single stroke for the lower, longer section of the acorn, pulling from the base upward. Use a no. 8 filbert to paint the cap of the acorn, pulling from the top down. Let dry completely.

5 Using a no. 8 shader, sideload one corner into Clear Medium. Work the medium into the brush by blending on the palette. Load the other corner into the dark brown mix and blend again. Shade the long section of the acorn where it meets the cap.

6 Thin Burnt Umber with Flow Medium and use a 10/0 liner to add the crosshatching to the caps. Paint the rest of the acorns around the candle holder the same way. Let dry.

7 Thin Burnt Umber with Flow Medium and use the no. 1 liner to paint rough, wiggly branches and stems. Follow the lines of the pattern and continue these around the candle holder, then let dry completely.

8 If desired, paint a leaf and two acorns on the top of the black wooden base as shown on page 76, using the same colors in acrylics instead of Enamels.

red contemporary
ceramic vase

materials

PAINTS
Burnt Umber
Burnt Sienna
Butter Pecan
Linen
Sunflower
Thicket
Warm White
Yellow Ochre

BRUSHES
nos. 8 and 10 shaders
nos. 6 and 10 filberts

SURFACE
"Red Passion" ceramic vase,
10¾-inches (27.3 cm) tall,
available from Pier 1 Imports.
Similar ceramic vases can be
found at home centers and
craft stores.

ADDITIONAL SUPPLIES
Clear Medium
Small plastic condiment or
storage cups to cover paint
mixes on your palette to keep
them moist.

The pale green-tinged cream flowers
"pop" against the warm red background of this tall, sleek,
ceramic vase. This combination creates a striking contemporary
accent for your table or mantle. Innovative brush-loading and
stroking techniques create the interesting striated petals.
I suggest displaying something simple in the vase, such as these
bare twigs, so the viewer's attention is drawn to the painting.

COLORS

Butter Pecan

Yellow Ochre

COLOR MIXES

CREAM MIX:
Warm White +
Linen 1:1

DARK OLIVE
GREEN MIX:
Thicket +
Burnt Sienna 2:1

LIGHT OLIVE
GREEN MIX:
Yellow Ochre + Dark
Olive Green mix 3:1

DARK BROWN MIX:
Burnt Sienna + Burnt
Umber 1:1

LIGHT YELLOW MIX:
Yellow Ochre + a touch
of Sunflower

LIGHT BROWN MIX:
Dark Brown mix +
Yellow Ochre 2:1

pattern

PREPARATION

Transfer only the flowers on the pattern using white transfer paper. The stems, leaves and branches are added freehand, following the pattern for placement.

1 Mix equal parts Warm White and Linen to make a cream mix. Using a no. 10 filbert, load one flat side in the cream mix, and the other flat side in Butter Pecan. Hold the brush so the Butter Pecan is to the right. Start at the outer tip of each petal and pull to the base, turning your brush so the Butter Pecan side faces the surface. Paint only the top three petals of each flower. Cover these colors on your palette to keep them moist; you'll paint the lower petals later.

2 Mix 2 parts Thicket and 1 part Burnt Sienna to make a dark olive green mix. Mix 1 part of this dark olive mix into 3 parts Yellow Ochre to make a light olive green. Thin a little of the light olive green with a drop of Clear Medium. Work Clear Medium into a no. 10 shader, pick up light olive and do a sideload float-shade at the base of the three white petals. Cover the green mixes to keep them moist. Mix equal parts Burnt Sienna and Burnt Umber to make a dark brown mix and basecoat the centers using a no. 6 filbert. Double load a no. 8 shader with the dark brown mix and Yellow Ochre and tap on the first layer of stamens. Add Sunflower to the Yellow Ochre for a light yellow mix, double load that and the brown mix, and tap on lighter stamens.

3 After the centers are dry, paint the lower two flower petals using the same brush and colors as for the top three petals. When these petals are dry, do a sideload float-shade of the base of the petals, just as you did in step 2 for the top petals. Double load a no. 10 shader with the dark olive green and light olive green. With the dark green corner of the brush toward the base of the flower, use the chisel edge to paint the stems with short overlapping strokes. Let dry and repeat if needed for more coverage. Using the same brush and colors, paint the large leaves with S-strokes. Switch to a no. 8 shader for the small leaves. Let dry.

4 Use a cotton swab to remove any remaining pattern lines. To paint the background twigs, load a no. 10 shader in the dark brown mix. Use the chisel edge to tap on rough lines starting at the top and continuing down among the flowers and leaves. Highlight the tips of the twigs by tapping on a light brown mix made up of the dark brown mix + Yellow Ochre. Let dry completely.

poinsettia christmas
ornaments

materials

PAINTS

Autumn Leaves

Baby Pink

Berry Wine

Burnt Sienna

Engine Red

Inca Gold Metallic

Italian Sage

Licorice

Pearl White Metallic

Rose Shimmer Metallic

Skin Tone

Thicket

Warm White

BRUSHES

nos. 6, 8 and 10 shaders

SURFACES

Beveled, frosted-glass ornaments in four different shapes (star, bell, tree and round) from Coopers' Works, 1360 Berryman Ave., Library, PA 15129; phone: 412-835-2441.

ADDITIONAL SUPPLIES

Clear Medium

Extender

Cotton swabs

Stylus

These frosted-glass ornaments painted

with shimmering pastel poinsettias will add sparkle and radiance to your Christmas décor. They have clear beveled edges and come in different holiday shapes such as a bell, a tree and a star. The round ornament also has a pretty gold wire decorative trim.

COLORS

Warm White	Inca Gold Metallic	Italian Sage	Rose Shimmer Metallic	Engine Red
Pearl White Metallic	Autumn Leaves			

COLOR MIXES

BLUSH MIX:
Skin Tone + Baby Pink 1:1

DARK BLUSH GLAZE MIX:
Blush mix + touch of Burnt Sienna + Clear Medium

DARK GREEN MIX:
Thicket + a speck of Licorice

MEDIUM GREEN MIX:
Italian Sage + a touch of Dark Green mix

RED MIX:
Engine Red + Autumn Leaves 1:1

DARK RED MIX:
Red mix + Berry Wine 1:1

REDDISH PINK MIX:
Red mix + Baby Pink 1:1

PALE PINK MIX:
Warm White + Baby Pink 2:1

SALMON MIX:
Baby Pink + Autumn Leaves 1:1

CREAMY WHITE MIX:
Warm White + a touch of Baby Pink

PALE ROSE METALLIC:
Pearl White Metallic + Rose Shimmer Metallic 1:1

LIGHT SAGE GREEN:
Italian Sage + Creamy White mix 1:1

pattern

This pattern may be hand-traced or photocopied for personal use only. It is shown here at 100%.

1 Tape the pattern to the back of your ornament. Place it a little off-center for a more interesting look. The ornaments I used for this project came already frosted. Load a no. 10 shader with Warm White and paint every other long petal first. There are 5 longer petals and 5 shorter ones.

2 Fill in the rest of the petals. Be sure to leave an open area in the center.

3 Mix Thicket + a speck of Licorice for a dark green mix; and Italian Sage + a touch of the dark green mix for a medium green. Double load a no. 8 shader in the dark green and the medium green. Stay up on the chisel edge, use very light pressure and tap in the needles for the evergreens, always keeping the dark green corner of the brush toward the center of the poinsettia. Start at the outside tip and work toward the center. To keep from getting too much paint on your brush, dab off both sides on the palette before going to your surface; this helps keep a sharp edge on your chisel. You can re-load from these dabs as well. The important thing is to use the paint very sparingly to make the evergreen needles.

4 Fill in with evergreens all around the petals, making some longer than others. Rotate the ornament as you move around the design to make painting more comfortable.

5 Double load a no. 8 shader in dark green mix on one corner, and Italian Sage on the other. Highlight each of the evergreen segments with a few light taps on the chisel edge, keeping the dark green corner toward the center of the poinsettia. Again, start at the outside edge of each evergreen branch and work toward the center, tucking in the needles as close as you can to the petals in the center.

6 For the first shade on the petals, mix equal parts Skin Tone and Baby Pink to make a blush mix. Create a sideload float using this blush mix and Clear Medium on a no. 10 shader. Pull your shader diagonally across each petal, starting at the left edge and pulling toward the base of each petal.

7 The first highlight on the upper left edge to the point of each petal is a sideload float of Warm White and Clear Medium on a no. 10 shader. The second shading is done on the upper right of each petal with the same sideload float as the first shading in step 6. Pull the no. 10 shader from the widest part of each petal up toward the outer tip.

8 For the second highlight, create a sideload float of Pearl White Metallic and Clear Medium and use the no. 10 shader to highlight the upper left edge again. To make the fine vein lines in the petals, darken the blush mix on your palette with a touch of Burnt Sienna and some Clear Medium to make a dark blush glaze mix. Use a no. 10 shader, stay up on the chisel edge, and tap the lines radiating up and outward from the base of each petal.

red poinsettia

9 For the poinsettia centers, use a regular cotton swab and the dark green mix to dot on the centers, then pick up a little Italian Sage on the edge of the swab and tap on highlights.

10 For the gold accents on the centers, use Inca Gold Metallic and tap on with a cotton swab. Finish the centers with a small dot of Autumn Leaves over the Inca Gold highlights. For the gold accents on the evergreen needles, tap Inca Gold Metallic lightly over the branches using the chisel edge of a sideloaded no. 8 shader.

11 Add accent dots of Inca Gold Metallic around the clear glass rim of the ornament using a stylus.

RED POINSETTIA: COLORS FOR PETALS, SHADING & HIGHLIGHTS

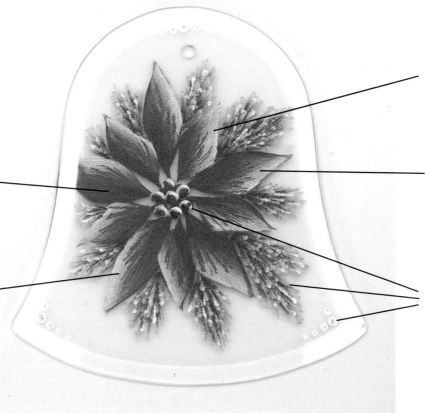

1. Petals: Red mix of equal parts Engine Red + Autumn Leaves.

2. Shade petals with a Dark Red mix of equal parts Red mix + Berry Wine.

3. Paint first highlight on petals with a Reddish pink mix of equal parts Red mix + Baby Pink.

4. Paint second highlight of Rose Shimmer Metallic over first highlight.

5. Lines on petals: Brush mix of Dark Red mix + Clear Medium; use the chisel edge of a no. 10 shader.

6. Centers, evergreens and gold dots are painted with the same colors and brushes as for the peach-tinted poinsettia. Follow Steps 3-5 and 9-11.

PINK POINSETTIA: COLORS FOR PETALS, SHADING & HIGHLIGHTS

1. Petals: Pale pink mix of Warm White + Baby Pink 2:1.

2. First Shade: Salmon mix of equal parts Baby Pink + Autumn Leaves.

3. Second Shade: Work Clear Medium into entire brush, pick up a speck of Engine Red on one corner, blend and apply over first shade.

4. First Highlight: Add a speck of Pale Pink mix to Warm White for a Creamy White mix and highlight the petals.

5. Second Highlight: Pale Rose Metallic mix of equal parts Pearl White Metallic + Rose Shimmer Metallic over first highlight.

6. Lines on petals: Brush mix Engine Red + Clear Medium; use the chisel edge of a no. 10 shader.

7. Centers, evergreens and gold dots are painted with the same colors and brushes as for the peach-tinted poinsettia. Follow Steps 3-5 and 9-11.

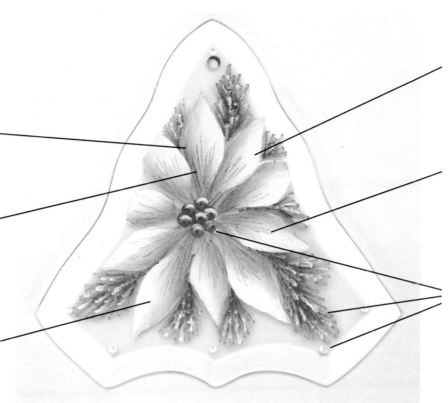

WHITE POINSETTIA: COLORS FOR PETALS, SHADING & HIGHLIGHTS

1. Petals: Make a Creamy White mix of Warm White + a touch of Baby Pink.

2. First Shade: Add an equal amount of Italian Sage to the Creamy White mix for a Light Sage mix. Dress a no. 10 flat in Clear Medium, sideload into the Light Sage mix. Shade the lower part and walk the color up into the petal. Use a no. 8 shader and deepen the shading in the narrower areas.

3. First Highlight: Creamy White mix on each petal.

4. Second Highlight: Pearl White Metallic over first highlight.

5. Prepare a Red Glaze: add a touch of Engine Red to Clear Medium. Dress a no. 10 flat in Clear Medium, sideload in Red Glaze, blend and apply to each petal.

6. Use chisel edge of no. 10 flat and Red Glaze for lines on petals.

7. Centers, evergreens and gold dots are painted with the same colors and brushes as for the peach-tinted poinsettia. Follow Steps 3-5 and 9-11.

daisies on
blue vase

materials

PAINTS

Burnt Sienna

Hauser Green Medium

Italian Sage

Thicket

Sunflower

Warm White

Yellow Ochre

BRUSHES

nos. 2 and 3 rounds

JS no. 1 liner

no. 2 filbert

nos. 4 and 6 shaders

SURFACE

Cobalt blue glass vase, 4¾-
inches (12.1cm) tall, found at a
flea market

ADDITIONAL SUPPLIES

Clear Medium

Flow Medium

Fine stylus

Wooden or bamboo skewer

This inexpensive blue glass flea-market find is transformed by the addition of a simple floral design. The pristine daisies look so fresh against the cobalt background while the yellow centers add just a touch of warmth. This motif is easily adaptable and would work just as well on both vintage cobalt bottles and contemporary glasses. In this project, the daisy design repeats five times around the widest part of the vase, and the daisy clusters are connected with simple green vines. Pop a few fresh daisies in it and place it on your breakfast table for a pretty, summery look.

COLORS

| Warm White | Burnt Sienna | Sunflower |

COLOR MIXES

DARK GREEN MIX:
Thicket + Hauser
Green Medium 3:2

YELLOW MIX:
Sunflower + Yellow
Ochre 2:1

MEDIUM GREEN MIX:
Italian Sage + Hauser
Green Medium 3:1

pattern

This pattern may be hand-traced or photocopied for personal use only. It is shown here at 100%. The pattern repeats five times around the circumference of the vase. Adjust the repeats to fit your own vase.

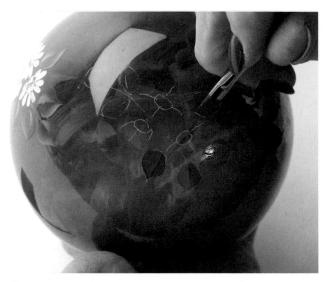

1 Trace and transfer the pattern to the outside of the vase with white transfer paper and a stylus. Trace only 3 or 4 petal lines for each daisy so your petal strokes will look more relaxed and natural. Mix 3 parts Thicket to 2 parts Hauser Green Medium on your palette to make a dark green. Undercoat the green leaves with a no. 6 shader and this dark green mix.

2 Using a no. 2 filbert and Warm White, undercoat each daisy center with one little stroke. Let dry.

3 With the no. 3 round and Warm White, begin pulling the individual petals of the large open daisy toward the center. Do the same for the other two daisies in the main cluster. Place the petals like a clockface, at 3, 6, 9 o'clock and 12 noon for the open daisy, and at 3, 9 and 12 noon for the others.

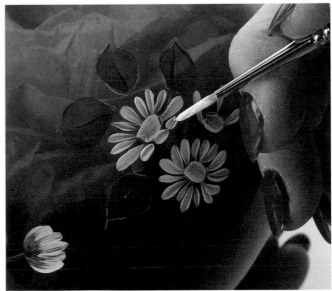

4 Fill in the rest of the petals on the large open daisy. Make some petals longer, some shorter, some wider and some thinner, just as in nature.

5 For the daisy that looks tipped over a little, paint the back petals the same as for the open daisy. For the foreshortened petals, stroke sideways three times starting at the left.

6 For the daisy that is opening, paint the petals the same way as for the tipped daisy, but make the petals more curved.

daisy centers, buds and leaves

7 Mix 2 parts Sunflower and 1 part Yellow Ochre to make the yellow basecoat mix for the centers. Paint this color over the white undercoat using the no. 2 filbert.

8 Switch to a no. 2 round and Warm White and paint the closed bud. Start with a comma stroke on each side, then fill in side-to-side with more comma strokes, then a straight stroke down the center. Let dry completely.

9 Mix 3 parts Italian Sage and 1 part Hauser Green Medium on your palette to make a medium green mix. Use a no. 6 shader for the larger leaves around the main daisy cluster and the no. 4 shader for the two leaves near the closed bud. Double load the no. 6 shader in dark green and medium green and paint two side-by-side strokes over the leaf undercoat color. Re-load between each stroke. If any of your leaves still look too sheer or if pattern lines are showing through, you can always repaint the leaves after the first coat is dry.

10 Work a tiny amount of Clear Medium into a no. 4 shader. Corner load in Burnt Sienna, blend, and shade each daisy center, referring to the photo for placement. Work a tiny amount of Clear Medium into a no. 4 shader. Corner load in Sunflower, blend, and highlight each daisy center in the area opposite the shaded area.

11 For the pollen dots, use a fine stylus and Sunflower thinned with Flow Medium. Re-load the stylus every four to five dots to get variation in dot size.

12 For the stems and vine, thin the medium green mix with a few drops of Flow Medium. Use a JS no. 1 liner and paint the stems. For the calyx on the closed bud, pull from the stem partway up onto the petals.

13 Connect the clusters around the vase with the vine. Use a cotton swab to remove any remaining pattern lines, and clean up any ragged edges with the point of a wooden or bamboo skewer.

hydrangeas on
glazed tile

materials

PAINTS

Burnt Umber

Calypso Sky

Hauser Green Medium

Hydrangea

Licorice

Periwinkle

Plum Vineyard

Sunflower

Thicket

Warm White

Yellow Ochre

BRUSHES

no. 2 round

nos. 4 and 10 shaders

nos. 4 and 6 filberts

JS no. 1 liner

SURFACES

6-inch (15.2cm) square, black glazed ceramic tile, available at home centers or local tile shops. Alderwood hand-crafted wooden box, black, #ACGN TB6B, available from BigCeramicStore.com.

ADDITIONAL SUPPLIES

Clear Medium

Flow Medium

Spongit Stick

What a lovely place to store your little treasures and keepsakes. The glazed black tile on this box creates a dramatic backdrop for the vibrant blue and lavender hydrangeas. The petals are painted with a technique that gives them a slight under-glow while a bit of tinting adds roundness and dimension to the blossoms. Finish the inside of the box with coordinating padded fabric or flocking to protect your keepsakes.

COLORS

| Warm White | Periwinkle | Yellow Ochre | Licorice |

COLOR MIXES

BRIGHT GREEN MIX:
Hauser Green Medium
+ Sunflower 1:1

DARK GREEN MIX:
Thicket + Bright Green
mix 3:1

GREEN GLAZE MIX:
Thicket + Hauser
Green Medium + Flow
Medium 2:1: drops

BLUE MIX:
Periwinkle + Calypso
Sky + Clear Medium
1:1:2

PLUM MIX:
Plum Vineyard + Burnt
Umber 2:1

**BRIGHT
YELLOW MIX:**
Yellow Ochre + a touch
of Sunflower

LIGHT BLUE MIX:
Hydrangea +
Periwinkle 1:1, thinned
with Flow Medium

pattern

PREPARATION

Use the Spongit Stick and Licorice to paint the white edge of the black tile. Let dry. Use well-worn white transfer paper to transfer as little of the pattern as possible to the black tile (only the shape of the flower heads and the base of the leaves). The ribbon and vines are painted with sheer paint that will not cover the tracing lines, so it is best to refer to the pattern to paint those. Or try placing a piece of plain paper between the pattern and the transfer paper to get the faintest possible tracing lines.

This pattern may be hand-traced or photocopied for personal use only. Enlarge at 133% to bring it up to full size.

1 To begin the leaves, mix equal parts Hauser Green Medium and Sunflower to make a bright green; mix 3 parts Thicket and 1 part of the bright green mix to make a dark green. Double load a no. 10 shader with these two greens, blend, and paint the leaves in two strokes, re-loading for the second stroke. On the first stroke, keep the light green to the middle of the leaf.

2 On the second stroke, keep the dark green to the middle; the contrast creates the indentation of the center vein. Turn the tile to a comfortable painting position so you can pull the strokes in the direction needed.

3 To begin the hydrangeas, mix 2 parts Thicket and 1 part Hauser Green Medium, and a few drops of Flow Medium to make a green glaze mix. Use a no. 6 filbert and fill in the area of each blossom. Work quickly and do not over-stroke. When the blossom areas are all filled in, let them dry before continuing.

4 Now working only on the blue hydrangea in the center, create a blue mix using equal parts Periwinkle and Calypso Sky, and 2 parts Clear Medium. Use this mix on a no. 4 filbert to begin the first layer of four-petal florets, overlapping the base of the leaves.

5 Continue filling in with this first layer, turning the tile as you work so the florets face outward all around the edges of the blossom.

6 Mix equal parts Periwinkle and Calypso Sky to make another puddle of blue mix (no Clear Medium this time). Add a puddle of Warm White to your palette. Using a no. 4 filbert, load one flat side in Warm White, and the other flat side in the blue mix. With the Warm White side toward the tile, paint four-petal florets randomly over the blossom area. Re-load for each floret.

7 Don't fill every last space of the blossom; allow the under-coat layer to show through in areas. Check that your blossom looks rounded around the outside edges and add florets if needed. Let dry.

lavender hydrangeas

8 For the lavender hydrangeas, begin the first layer of florets using a mix of 1 part Periwinkle + 2 parts Clear Medium. Use a no. 4 filbert and loosely paint these florets in, overlapping the leaves and allowing the undercoat green glaze to show through in some areas.

9 Continue filling in with this first layer of florets to create the shape of the blossom. This is a side view of a hydrangea so the shape is not as rounded; it's more of a half circle or umbrella shape. Let dry.

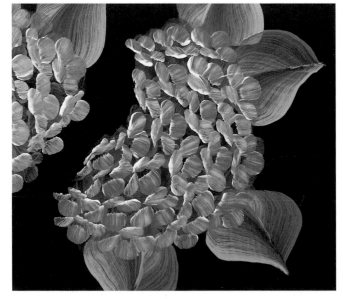

10 With straight Periwinkle on one side of a no. 4 filbert, and Warm White on the other side, begin the next layer of florets on the lavender hydrangea. Keep the Warm White side of the brush toward the tile and paint the florets randomly over the first layer. Let dry completely.

11 Mix a tinting color with 2 parts Plum Vineyard and 1 part Burnt Umber to make a plum mix. Work a little Clear Medium into the no. 4 shader, sideload into the plum mix, and float this tinting color onto the floret petals around the outside of the hydrangea blossoms.

12 Tinting shades the blossoms and gives them a rounded look and also enriches and deepens the colors.

13 For the centers of the florets, use the dark green mix and the point of a no. 2 round to stipple in a center on every floret. Mix in a touch of Clear Medium to a puddle of Yellow Ochre. Use the tip of the no. 2 round to dot a yellow center on only the florets that have been tinted with the plum mix in steps 11 and 12. Add a touch of Sunflower to the Yellow Ochre to make a bright yellow mix and dot on the yellow centers on the brightest, untinted florets in the centers of the blossoms.

14 The sheer blue ribbons are painted with the same blue mix you used in step 4 for the first layer of florets. Use a no. 10 shader and paint two connecting S-strokes for the tails of the ribbons extending below the hydrangeas.

15 Detail the front edge of each ribbon with equal parts Hydrangea and Periwinkle, thinned with a little Flow Medium to make a light blue mix. Load a no. 1 liner in this color and pull a long smooth line that connects the two S-strokes. Don't forget to paint the two short connecting ribbons between the hydrangeas.

16 Use a no. 1 liner to paint the subtle background vines, and the no. 4 shader to paint the little leaves, using the green glaze mix from step 3. Let dry completely before placing the tile into the lid of the wooden keepsake box.

bellflowers on
candle holder

materials

PAINTS

Autumn Leaves

Burnt Sienna

Burnt Umber

Cobalt

Italian Sage

Skin Tone

Sunflower

Thicket

Yellow Ochre

BRUSHES

nos. 5 and 6 rounds

no. 6 shader

JS no. 1 liner

SURFACE

Rectangular glass candle holder, 9 inches (22.9 cm) wide x 4½ inches (11.5 cm) high x 4 inches (10.2 cm) deep, available from Wal-Mart.

ADDITIONAL SUPPLIES

Clear Medium

Flow Medium

Stylus

This heavy glass candle holder is worthy

of a place on your mantle or shelf where it can be admired at eye level. Once you learn to paint these bellflowers, I know you will want to try different color options. All you need is a round brush and three values of your favorite color. Each bellflower is easy to paint using the fan stroke you learned on page 15. The secret is to keep the front of the bellflower lighter in color than the back to achieve the round, trumpet shape of the petal. Choose a candle color that contrasts with or shows off the colors of your flowers.

COLOR MIXES

DARK GREEN MIX:
Thicket + Burnt Umber
+ Cobalt 4:1:1

DARK CORAL MIX:
Autumn Leaves +
Burnt Sienna 3:1

MEDIUM CORAL MIX:
Skin Tone + a touch of
Dark Coral mix

LIGHT CORAL MIX:
Medium Coral mix +
a touch of Skintone +
Clear Medium

MEDIUM YELLOW MIX:
Yellow Ochre +
Sunflower 3:2

MEDIUM GREEN MIX:
Italian Sage + a touch
of Dark Green mix

LIGHT GREEN MIX:
Italian Sage + a touch
of Sunflower

patterns

Left side

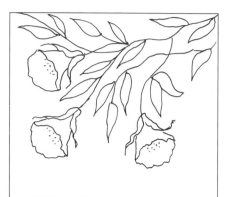

Right side

These patterns may be hand-traced or photocopied for personal use only. Enlarge the Left and Right side patterns at 172%, and the Long side pattern at 185%, to bring them up to full size.

PREPARATION
Transfer the patterns to white bond paper; cut them to fit your candle holder and tape them face out to the inside surface.

Long side

1 Begin with the right side of the candle holder. Mix 4 parts Thicket, 1 part Burnt Umber, 1 part Cobalt and a few drops of Flow Medium to make a dark green. Paint the vines and stems with the no. 1 liner.

2 Mix 3 parts Autumn Leaves and 1 part Burnt Sienna to make a dark coral. Mix a touch of this dark coral color into a small puddle of Skin Tone to make a medium coral. Fully load a no. 6 round with the dark coral mix. Tip into the medium coral and swirl the brush tip in the puddle. Touch the tip to the palette to remove excess. Starting with the back petal of the bellflower, press the brush to the glass surface and pause to let the bristles splay out, wiggling the brush slightly to help them open up to fill out the petal outline on the pattern.

3 Lift the ferrule slightly and push the bristles forward a little to bring them up to the pattern line. Compare the position of the bristles in this photo with their position in Step 2.

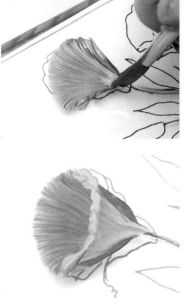

4 Pull the bristles back as you release pressure on them and lift up to the point. You have now formed the back petal of the bellflower. Repeat Steps 2, 3 and 4 for the rest of the bellflowers on this side of the candle holder. Let dry before going on to the next step.

5 Add a touch of Skin Tone to the medium coral mix, plus a bit of Clear Medium to make a light coral. Create the front part of the bell-flower using a no. 5 round. Pick up a generous amount of this light coral mix on the tip of the brush. Dribble a crescent-shape line across the lower middle of the back petal to create the top edge of the front petal. Remove excess paint from the brush by wiping across a paper towel.

6 Catch this line with the tip of the no. 5 round and pull down toward the base of the bellflower, repeating until the entire front of the bellflower has been filled in. Repeat Steps 5 and 6 for the rest of the bellflowers on this side of the candle holder. Let dry.

7 Mix 3 parts Yellow Ochre and 2 parts Sunflower plus a touch of Clear Medium to make a medium yellow. Use a stylus to dot on yellow pollen dots in the throat of each bellflower. To paint the single-stroke leaves, use the dark green mix you used for the vines; make a medium green by adding a touch of dark green to Italian Sage; make a light green by adding a touch of Sunflower to Italian Sage. Double load the no. 6 shader into the dark green, and either the medium green or light green for variation in leaf color. Wipe the brush lightly over a paper towel when you change colors.

8 To paint the calyx, load the no. 1 liner into the dark green mix and pull the bristles across the top of the puddle of the medium green or the light green to vary the colors. Pull a line up from the point of the bellflower base on both sides, wig-gling the line and pulling to a point.

9 Paint the other two sides of the glass candle holder to finish. Tape the patterns on page 104 to the inside and use the same colors and brushes.

flowering herb
tile coasters

materials

PAINTS

Burnt Umber

Hauser Green Medium

Italian Sage

Lemon Custard

Licorice

Periwinkle

Plum Pudding

Raw Sienna

Rose Garden

Rose Pink

Thicket

Warm White

Wicker White

BRUSHES

nos. 2, 4, 6 and 10 shaders

10/0 shader

nos. 2 and 4 filberts

no. 4 round

JS no. 1 liner

SURFACES

Four "Rialto Beige" ceramic
tiles, 3½ inches (8.9 cm)
square, from Home Depot

ADDITIONAL SUPPLIES

Medium grit sandpaper

Rubbing alcohol

Paper towels

Ruler or small T-square

Blue painter's tape

Krylon Matte Spray Finish

FolkArt Outdoor Satin Sealer

These herb tiles would make charming accents in a Tuscan or country kitchen, whether displayed on a wall, lining a tray or used as coasters. Unlike glass, the tile surface is porous, so use regular acrylic paints. A topcoat of outdoor satin sealer makes them durable.

COLORS

Burnt Umber

Rose Garden

Rose Pink

Warm White

Raw Sienna

Italian Sage

Lemon Custard

COLOR MIXES

LEAF GREEN MIX:
Thicket + a touch of
Burnt Umber

DARK GREEN MIX:
Thicket + a touch of
Licorice

DARK PLUM MIX:
Plum Pudding + a
touch of Periwinkle

LIGHT PLUM MIX:
Warm White + a touch
of Dark Plum mix

DULL GREEN MIX:
Thicket + Rose Garden
4:1

PALE PINK MIX:
Wicker White + a
speck of Rose Garden

WARM ROSE MIX:
Rose Garden + a touch
of Raw Sienna

OLIVE GREEN MIX:
Dull Green mix +
Lemon Custard 1:1

BROWN MIX:
Raw Sienna + Burnt
Umber 1:1

SAGE GREEN MIX:
Italian Sage + Hauser
Green Medium 2:1

**MEDIUM LEAF
GREEN MIX:**
Hauser Green Medium
+ a touch of Thicket

patterns

These patterns may be hand-traced or photocopied for personal use only. Enlarge at 106% to bring them up to full size.

PREPARATION
Use medium grit sandpaper to scuff the surface of the tiles so the paint will adhere better. Clean with rubbing alcohol on a paper towel.

1 Before transferring the pattern, you'll need to "antique" the tile. If you're painting all four tiles, it's easier to antique all of them at the same time so they're dry and ready for painting. Use a small T-square or ruler and a pencil to mark off ½-Inch (13mm) from each edge of the tile; tape off the ½-inch (13mm) border with blue painter's tape. Burnish the tape along the inside edges to prevent paint seepage.

2 Moisten the top of the tile with a brush and clean water. Pick up Burnt Umber acrylic paint on a "pounce pad" (a wadded up, damp paper towel), off-load excess paint on your palette, and pounce on the Burnt Umber while the tile is still moist. Start at the edges and work toward the center. The antiquing should be more pronounced around three corners, fading off at the fourth corner and in the center where the flowers and stems will be painted.

3 Remove the painter's tape before the paint dries and erase any visible pencil marks.

4 With a dampened no. 10 shader, sideload into Burnt Umber and antique the tile's rough edges. Let dry. Spray with Krylon Matte Finish to protect the paint from being lifted off as you work.

chives

1 Transfer the "Chives" pattern onto the center antiqued area of the tile. If you will be painting the lettering too, transfer the lettering on the pattern now. Load a no. 2 filbert with Rose Garden acrylic paint and basecoat the chive blossoms with a tapping motion of the chisel edge to get a spiky, uneven look. Load one flat side of the no. 2 filbert in Rose Garden and the other flat side in Rose Pink acrylic paint. Use the chisel edge to tap on the next layer of spiky petals.

2 Load the no. 2 filbert, one flat side in Rose Pink and the other in Warm White. Use the chisel edge to tap on the highlights in the center areas of each blossom. The buds are painted with the no. 4 filbert double loaded with Rose Garden and Rose Pink, with the Rose Pink side of the brush toward the tile. Add a small highlight to the buds with Warm White. Use a no. 10 shader and a sideload float of Raw Sienna to shade the base of each blossom.

3 To paint the root end of the chive cluster, load a no. 4 round in Warm White, tip into Raw Sienna and pull upward from the base of the root with three overlapping strokes. Shade the base with a sideload float of Raw Sienna on a no. 10 shader.

4 The chive leaves and stems are painted with a leaf green mix of Thicket + a touch of Burnt Umber. Use a no. 10 shader and stay up on the chisel edge to paint the fine lines. Pull them from the outer tip down into the root end. Use a no. 1 liner and the leaf green mix to extend the green leaves into the base. Extend the shading of the base upward using the liner and Raw Sienna.

5 Paint the lettering on two sides of the tile using a 10/0 shader and a dark green mix of Thicket + a touch of Licorice. Let dry completely. Seal the tile with Outdoor Satin Sealer to protect the painting from moisture.

1 Transfer the "Lavender" pattern onto the tile. With a dark green mix of Thicket + a touch of Licorice, use a no. 1 liner to paint the stems. Make a dark plum mix of Plum Pudding + a touch of Periwinkle. Make a light plum mix using a touch of the dark plum mix + Warm White. Use a no. 2 filbert loaded one flat side in the dark plum and the other flat side in the light plum mix. Stay up on the chisel edge and tap on the first layer of fan-shaped lavender blossoms.

2 Highlight the blossoms with the light plum mix on one side of the no. 2 filbert.

3 Use a no. 10 shader to add a sideload float of the dark plum mix to the base of each lavender blossom. Add tiny sepals at the base with Burnt Umber on a no. 1 liner.

4 Paint the leaves with a no. 1 liner. Double load the liner in the dark green mix of Thicket + a touch of Licorice, and in a lighter green of Italian Sage thinned with a little water. Pull each leaf in toward the stem.

5 Paint the lettering on two sides of the tile using a 10/0 shader and a dark green mix of Thicket + a touch of Licorice. Let dry completely. Seal the tile with Outdoor Satin Sealer to protect it from moisture.

oregano

1 Transfer the pattern onto the tile. Mix a dull green with 4 parts Thicket and 1 part Rose Garden. Use a no. 1 liner and paint the stems. Shade the stems where they meet the flowers with Raw Sienna on the no. 1 liner.

2 Mix Wicker White + a speck of Rose Garden to make a pale pink. Load a no. 2 filbert in pale pink on one flat side, and the other flat side in Rose Garden. Use the chisel edge and tap on the tiny petals of the oregano blossom.

3 Mix a touch of Raw Sienna into Rose Garden to make a warm rose mix and do a sideload float for the first shading of the base of the blossoms. The second shading is a sideload float of Raw Sienna.

4 To paint the leaves, mix equal parts of the dull green mix + Lemon Custard to make an olive green mix. Load one corner of a no. 2 shader into the dull green mix and the other corner into the olive green mix, and blend. Paint the small single stroke leaves. The medium leaves are done with a no. 4 shader, and the largest leaves with the no. 6 shader.

5 Paint the lettering on two sides of the tile using a 10/0 shader and a dark green mix of Thicket + a touch of Licorice. Let dry completely. Seal the tile with Outdoor Satin Sealer to protect from moisture.

1 Mix equal parts Raw Sienna and Burnt Umber to make a brown mix. Mix 2 parts Italian Sage + 1 part Hauser Green Medium to make a sage green mix. Load one flat side of a no. 10 shader into the brown, and the other side into the sage green. Paint the stems using the chisel edge of the brush. For the blossoms, paint the first layer with a dark plum mix of Plum Pudding + a touch of Periwinkle on one flat side of a no. 2 shader, and Warm White on the other side. Each petal is a tiny comma stroke; the top petals are leaf strokes.

2 With Lemon Custard sideloaded on a no. 4 shader, float highlights on some of the lighter areas on the petals. With the same colors used for the stems in Step 1, load one flat side of a no. 2 shader in the brown mix and the other flat side in the sage green mix and add tiny dried leaves above some of the petals.

3 The large leaves are painted with a medium leaf green mix of Hauser Green Medium + a touch of Thicket on one side of a no. 6 shader, and a sage green mix on the other side. For some of the leaves, keep the medium leaf green side to the surface; for others turn the sage green side to the surface. Highlight some leaves with a sheer sideload float of Lemon Custard. Shade some of the leaves with a sheer sideload float of dark green mix. Use a no. 1 liner and thinned brown mix to add the leaf stems and center veins.

4 Paint the lettering on two sides of the tile using a 10/0 shader and a dark green mix of Thicket + a touch of Licorice. Let dry completely. Seal the tile with Outdoor Satin Sealer to protect from moisture.

three-tier
berry bowls

materials

PAINTS

Autumn Leaves

Berry Wine

Burnt Sienna

Burnt Umber

Fresh Foliage

Hydrangea

Italian Sage

Midnight

Periwinkle

Plum Vineyard

Purple Lilac

Thicket

Warm White

BRUSHES

nos. 4, 6 and 8 shaders

no. 2 round

JS no. 1 liner

no. 4 filbert

SURFACES

3-tiered white china serving
bowls by B. Smith With Style
Home Collection, available at
Bed Bath & Beyond

ADDITIONAL SUPPLIES

Detail Painter (small)

Cotton swabs, nonfuzzy, from
beauty supply stores

Clear Medium

Flow Medium

These white china bowls are just the right size
for serving fresh berries for a cool ice-cream and berry dessert,
or maybe little tea cookies, even candies and after-dinner mints.
Their clean, white color gives you lots of options for painting.
Choose three kinds of berries for a summery look. In this project,
blackberries, raspberries and blueberries encircle each bowl
with vines and leaves. A set of handpainted bowls like these
would make an extra-special gift for a bride, or a lovely house-
warming gift for a new homeowner.

COLORS

Midnight

Purple Lilac

Italian Sage

Warm White

Fresh Foliage

Burnt Umber

Plum Vineyard

COLOR MIXES

PURPLE MIX:
Midnight + Berry Wine
+ medium 1:1:2

PALE LILAC MIX:
Purple Lilac (thinned) +
Warm White

DARK GREEN MIX:
Thicket + a touch of
Burnt Umber

BERRY RED MIX:
Autumn Leaves +
Berry Wine 3:2

RASPBERRY MIX:
Berry Wine + Autumn
Leaves 2:1

DARK RED MIX:
Berry Wine + Burnt
Sienna 1:1

LIGHT RED MIX:
Berry Red mix + Warm
White + Clear Medium

HIGHLIGHT MIX:
Light Red mix + more
Warm White

MEDIUM BLUE MIX:
Hydrangea + Peri-
winkle 1:1

LIGHT BLUE MIX:
Hydrangea + a touch
of Periwinkle

patterns

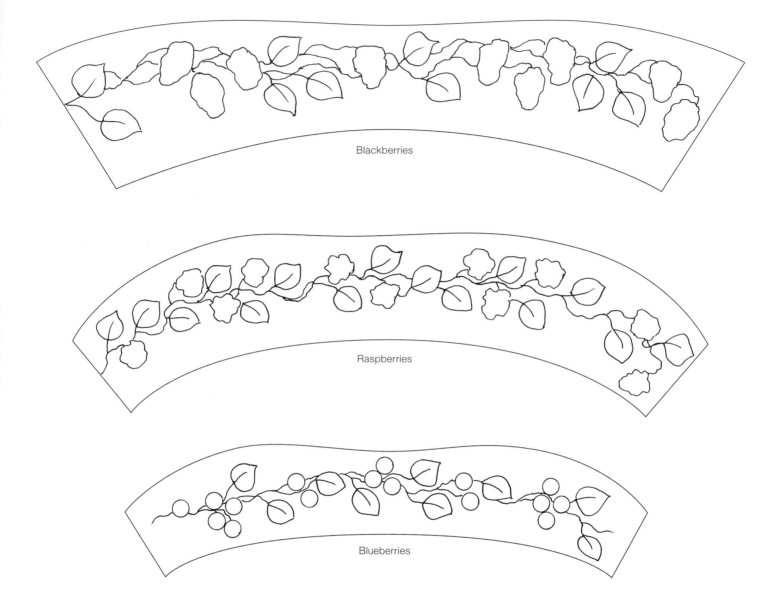

Blackberries

Raspberries

Blueberries

These patterns may be hand-traced or photocopied for personal use only. Enlarge each pattern at 156% to bring them up to full size.

PREPARATION

Transfer the pattern to one side of the bowl. Repeat for the other side. The dip in the pattern's outer edge reflects the dip in the sides of the bowls used in this demo. It's best to transfer just the berries and to paint the large leaves by referring to the pattern for placement. The small, light leaves and vines are painted freehand.

1 Transfer just the berries on the pattern to the bowl, then refer to the pattern for the placement of the leaves and vines. With Midnight on a dry cotton swab, dot on each individual segment of the berry to fill in the pattern. When the berries are filled in with this first color, tint them with a purple mix of 1 part Berry Wine, 1 part Midnight and 2 parts Clear Medium. Use a no. 6 shader. Compare the two berries on the right with the untinted one on the left to see how the color deepens when you tint.

2 Shade the lower left of each berry with Midnight sideloaded on a no. 6 shader that's been dressed in Clear Medium. Highlight the segments in the upper right of each berry with Purple Lilac sideloaded on a no. 6 shader dressed in Clear Medium.

3 The final, brightest highlight in the shaded area (lower left) of each berry is Purple Lilac thinned with Clear Medium. Use a stylus to dot this color on the upper right of each little round segment. The final highlight on the segments in the upper right of the berries is done with a mix of thinned Purple Lilac + Warm White to make a pale lilac mix. Use the liner to dot these on; they're a little bigger and brighter than the highlights in the shaded portion.

4 The leaves and vines are painted in to connect the berries all around the bowl. Mix Thicket and a touch of Burnt Umber to make a dark green. Double load a no. 8 shader with the dark green mix and Italian Sage, and paint the large leaves with two side-by-side strokes. Thin a small amount of Burnt Umber with Flow Medium. Use a no. 1 liner to paint the vines. Thin Italian Sage with Flow Medium to make a sheer green. Paint the sheer stems with a no. 1 liner, and the sheer leaves with a no. 4 or 6 shader.

raspberries

1 Transfer only the berries on the pattern to the bowl. Mix 3 parts Autumn Leaves and 2 parts Berry Wine to make a berry red mix. Dot this color on with a cotton swab to form each segment of the raspberry. Tint the berries with a mix of 2 parts Berry Wine and 1 part Autumn Leaves, thinned with Clear Medium, to make a raspberry mix. Use a no. 6 shader. To create some unripe segments on a few of the berries, use Fresh Foliage on a brush dressed in Clear Medium to add a slight green tinge.

2 Mix equal parts Berry Wine and Burnt Sienna to make a dark red mix. Shade the lower left of the berries using a side-load float.

3 The first highlight is done with a light red mix made up of the berry red mix + Warm White, with a few drops of Clear Medium. Highlight the upper right of the fully-ripe berry. Add Clear Medium to the light red mix and use a stylus to add highlight dots to the lower left of each berry. Add more Warm White to that mix to make a highlight mix and highlight all the berries in the upper right segments.

4 The leaves and vines are painted in to connect the berries all around the bowl. Mix Thicket and a touch of Burnt Umber to make a dark green. Double load a no. 6 shader with the dark green mix and Italian Sage and paint the large leaves with two side-by-side strokes. Thin a small amount of Burnt Umber with Flow Medium. Use a no. 1 liner to paint the vines. Thin Italian Sage with Flow Medium to make a sheer green. Paint the sheer stems with a no. 1 liner, and the sheer leaves with a no. 4 or 6 shader.

1 Transfer only the berries on the pattern to the bowl. Mix equal parts Hydrangea and Periwinkle to make a medium blue mix. Load a small detail painter in this color and paint each berry with a touch, twist, and lift motion. Tint some of the berries with Plum Vineyard thinned with Clear Medium on a no. 4 filbert.

2 Shade each blueberry on the lower left with a sideload float of Midnight.

3 The soft highlight along the upper right curve of each berry is done with a sideload float of the light blue mix (Hydrangea + a touch of Periwinkle). The final highlights are dotted on with the tip of a no. 2 round brush and Warm White thinned with a little Clear Medium.

4 The leaves and vines are painted in to connect the berries all around the bowl. Mix Thicket and a touch of Burnt Umber to make a dark green. Double load a no. 6 shader with the dark green mix and Italian Sage and paint the large leaves with two side-by-side strokes. Thin a small amount of Burnt Umber with Flow Medium. Use a no. 1 liner to paint the vines. Thin Italian Sage with Flow Medium to make a sheer green. Paint the sheer stems with a no. 1 liner, and the sheer leaves with a no. 4 or 6 shader.

elegant floral china
place setting

materials

PAINTS

Autumn Leaves

Berry Wine

Burnt Sienna

Cobalt

Hauser Green Medium

Inca Gold Metallic

Italian Sage

Metallic Gold

Periwinkle

Sunflower

Thicket

Yellow Ochre

Warm White

Wicker White

BRUSHES

nos. 2 and 4 shaders

no. 1 round

no. 1 liner

nos. 2 and 4 filberts

JS 10/0 liner

SURFACES

"Simona" white porcelain charger, dinner plate and oval napkin ring, available from Maryland China Co.

ADDITIONAL SUPPLIES

Clear Medium

Flow Medium

Spongit Sticks

Stylus

Turntable or lazy susan

With these exquisite porcelain pieces, the multi-hued floral designs and the gold accents, you can add grace and flair to your dining table. The colorful flowers seem almost casual when you look at them closely, yet the total effect is truly elegant.

COLORS

Thicket	Autumn Leaves	Hauser Green Medium	Italian Sage	Wicker White

COLOR MIXES

GOLD MIX: Inca Gold Metallic + Metallic Gold 1:1

RED MIX: Berry Wine + Autumn Leaves + Burnt Sienna 1:1: a touch

PINK MIX: Warm White + a touch of Red mix

DARK BLUE MIX: Periwinkle + Cobalt 3:1

LIGHT BLUE MIX: Warm White + a touch of Dark Blue mix

YELLOW MIX: Sunflower + Yellow Ochre 2:1

LIGHT YELLOW MIX: Yellow mix + a touch of Warm White + Clear Medium

To paint the coordinating porcelain napkin rings, follow the instructions for Garland #1 on pages 124 and 125. Outline the edges with the gold mix.

patterns

Garland #1: red roses, blue forget-me-nots & orange daisies

Garland #2: red roses, blue bellflowers & orange foxgloves

NAPKIN RING

Red roses, blue forget-me-nots & orange daisies

These patterns may be hand-traced or photocopied for personal use only. They are shown here at 100%. Trace and transfer only the outline of the roses on the pattern to the charger. Refer to the patterns for all other details.

gold rim on dinner plate and charger

1 With a gold mix of equal parts Inca Gold Metallic and Metallic Gold loaded on a Spongit Stick, apply gold paint to the rim of the plate by holding the sponge stick against the rim as you slowly turn the turntable or lazy susan.

2 Re-load your Spongit Stick with the gold paint every few inches. Continue around the rim to your starting point, marked by a china marker. Let dry and apply two more coats, letting dry between each coat.

3 With the same gold mix plus a touch of Flow Medium, paint a repeating design of comma strokes and dip dots, following the shape of the rim of your plate. Use a no. 1 liner and a stylus.

4 If you wish, add a tassel design to the rim of the dinner plate and charger. Add a touch of Wicker White to Clear Medium. Dress the no. 1 round in this mix, then swirl the tip of the brush in the gold mix and make a fan-stroke tassel at each three-dot mark. Let dry completely.

rose garlands on rim of charger

1 The rose garlands demonstrated on these two pages are painted only on the rim of the charger. The dinner plate is set on top of the charger and protects the painted designs from food and scrapes (see the photo on page 120). Using the patterns as reference, start with the large pink roses in the center of each garland. Mix equal parts Berry Wine + Autumn Leaves, plus a touch of Burnt Sienna to make a red mix. Add a touch of this red mix to Warm White to make a pink mix. Double load a no. 4 shader with these two mixes. Holding the brush so the pink side is to the plate, paint the three back petals of the rose.

2 With the same brush and colors, paint the two petals at the front of the bowl of the rose. For the second petal, turn the brush so the red is to the surface.

3 Add the tiny petals under the right and left sides of the bowl of the rose with tiny dabs of paint.

4 Paint all the roses around the charger rim the same way. Each garland has two roses. Load a no. 2 filbert with the same red and pink mixes and apply a single stroke rosebud on each side of the open roses. Let dry.

5 Thin Thicket with a little Flow Medium and use a 10/0 liner to paint the calyxes on each rose bud, plus a short stem. Load a no. 4 shader with straight Thicket and add the four green two-stroke leaves around the roses. Finally, use a 10/0 liner and thinned Thicket to place the vines extending out on each side of the rose clusters.

6 Garland #1: Mix 3 parts Periwinkle and 1 part Cobalt to make a dark blue mix; add a touch of this dark blue to Warm White to make a light blue mix. Double load a no. 2 filbert with these two mixes. Turn the charger to a comfortable painting position. Keeping the light blue side of the brush to the surface, paint the blue flowers that extend out from the side of the roses. The yellow centers are dotted on with a fine stylus and a yellow mix of 2 parts Sunflower and 1 part Yellow Ochre thinned with Flow Medium.

7 Garland #2: With the same dark and light blue mixes, paint blue bellflowers on garland #2 on the rim of the charger.

8 Garland #1: Mix 2 parts Sunflower and 1 part Yellow Ochre to make a yellow mix, but do not add Flow Medium. Double load a no. 2 filbert in the yellow mix on one side and Autumn Leaves on the other and use the chisel edge to paint the orange daisies—one full one, and a couple of partial ones—on the other side of the garland from the blue flowers in Step 6. Dot in the centers with Hauser Green Medium.

9 Garland #2: Using a no. 2 shader and the same color mixes as for the daisies, paint the orange foxgloves on the other side of garland #2. Begin with a single stroke, with the yellow mix toward the surface.

10 Garland #2: Come back with a sideload float of the light yellow mix to form the trumpet of the foxgloves.

11 For both garlands, use the no. 4 shader to add a sideload float of the red mix inside the bowl of each rose. Pollen dots are the yellow mix + Flow Medium. Fill in with leaves, referring to the patterns. Use Thicket on a no. 4 shader for the small single-stroke leaves. Load a no. 2 filbert with Italian Sage and paint the small, sheer leaves. Thin Thicket with Flow Medium and use a 10/0 liner for the comma strokes. Repeat the garlands around the rim, alternating them as you go for more interest.

where to find it

U.S. RETAILERS

Surfaces:
Most of the surfaces in this book were purchased at national chain stores (or their websites) such as Bed Bath & Beyond, Linens 'N Things, Michaels, A.C. Moore, Crate & Barrel, Pottery Barn, Pier 1 Imports, Wal-Mart and Home Depot. For vintage china and glassware, explore flea markets and estate sales, or search on eBay.

Paints:
FolkArt Enamel & Acrylic Paints:
Plaid Enterprises, Inc.
3225 Westech Drive
Norcross, GA 30092
www.plaidonline.com

Brushes:
Loew-Cornell
400 Sylvan Avenue
Englewood Cliffs, NJ 07632
www.loew-cornell.com

EtchAll Dip 'n Etch:
B & B Etching Products, Inc.
19721 N. 98th Ave.
Peoria, AZ 85382
Ph. 888-382-4255
www.etchall.com

Matte Finish Spray and 18 kt. Gold Leafing Pen:
Krylon
1-800-KRYLON
www.krylon.com

Kreative Kanvas:
The Kunin Group
www.kuningroup.com

Beveled Glass Ornaments:
Coopers' Works
1360 Berryman Avenue
Library, Pa 15129
Ph. 412-835-2441

Black Alderwood Tile Box:
881 E. Glendale
Sparks, NV 89431
www.BigCeramicStore.com
Ph. 888-513-5303

Porcelain Dinner Plate, Charger and Oval Napkin Ring:
Maryland China Co., Inc.
54 Main St.
Reisterstown, MD 21136
www.marylandchina.com
Ph. 410-833-5559

Cobalt Blue Wine Glasses:
Available only online at
www.target.com

Patterns and instructions for Rooster Plate and Napkin Ring shown on page 32:
Arlene Swiatek Gillen
P.O. Box 172
Holland, NY 14080
e-mail: arlene.gillen@roadrunner.com

CANADIAN RETAILERS

Crafts Canada
120 North Archibald St.
Thunder Bay, ON P7C 3X8
Tel: 888-482-5978
www.craftscanada.ca

Folk Art Enterprises
P.O. Box 1088
Ridgetown, ON, N0P 2C0
Tel: 800-265-9434

MacPherson Arts & Crafts
91 Queen St. E., P.O. Box 1810
St. Mary's, ON, N4X 1C2
Tel: 800-238-6663
www.macphersoncrafts.com

The best in painting instruction & inspiration
is from North Light Books!

Handpainted Tiles for Your Home

Handpainted Tiles for Your Home features over 20 fabulous step-by-step projects for transforming ordinary ceramic floor and wall tiles into charming decorative accents. From address tiles and trivets to serving trays and tin ceiling tiles, you'll find fresh ideas and creative inspiration for all types of personal tastes, including today's favorite decorating themes such as wine country accents, Tuscan-inspired motifs, and French country designs. Tiles of all kinds are inexpensive and easy to find at any home improvement center, and with acrylic paints and sealers, no firing is required!
ISBN-13: 978-1-58180-641-0, ISBN-10: 1-58180-641-8, paperback, 128 pages, #33227

The Brushstroke Handbook

The Brushstroke Handbook is your complete reference for mastering more than 50 fabulous strokes using both round and flat brushes. In hundreds of clear and colorful photos, master decorative artist and teacher Maureen McNaughton breaks each stroke down into small movements so you can perfect your brushwork with ease. You'll see how to combine strokes to create gorgeous flowers, birds, butterflies, lace, ribbons and more. Bonus sections on painting fresh and pretty borders plus six lovely compositions put your new-found expertise to work. The lay-flat spiral binding makes it easy to flip through and find the brushstroke you want—instantly!
ISBN-13: 978-1-58180-782-0; ISBN-10: 1-58180-782-1; hardcover, 144 pages, #33451

Donna Dewberry's Designs for Entertaining

Make your home look festive and inviting for every occasion with *Donna Dewberry's Designs for Entertaining*. This inspiring guide blends more than 60 easy, one-stroke painting projects with fabulous decorating ideas and spectacular table settings. From trays and glassware to tablecloths and candleholders, Donna lends her popular painting style to a range of surfaces, and even shares her own special recipes and party tips. You'll learn step-by-step how to paint on everyday dinnerware, party plates, and even crystal stemware for those extra-special occasions!
ISBN-13: 978-1-58180-799-8, ISBN-10: 1-58180-799-6, paperback, 160 pages, #33477

Fast & Fun Flowers in Acrylics

Popular artist Lauré Paillex shows you everything you need to create fun, bright and colorful flowers of all kinds! You'll find more than 60 step-by-step demonstrations that give you great results in a jiffy. No demo is more than six steps long, and the convenient lay-flat spiral binding makes this a book you'll keep open on your painting table for quick reference any time. From garden flowers to wildflowers, from spring bulbs to roses and orchids, you'll find just the flower you need for any project—or just for the fun of painting!
ISBN-13: 978-1-58180-827-8, ISBN-10: 1-58180-827-5, hardcover, 128 pages, #33503